May Kare
story be
as much a
life blessed w
Remember that
and your ch
loves you
he hears
and he saves
(Psalm 56:8)

Your prayer
Your tears,

Robin

Baby Karen's Gift

Baby
Karen's Gift

Robin Young Goza

Belleville, Ontario, Canada

Baby Karen's Gift
Copyright © 2002, Robin Young Goza

Scriptures marked KJV are from *the Holy Bible, Authorized King James Version*, Harper and Brothers Publishers.

Scriptures marked AMP are from the *Amplified Bible*, copyright © 1965 by Zondervan Publishing House.

Scriptures marked NASB are from the *New American Standard Bible*, copyright © 1960, 1977 by the Lockman Foundation.

Scriptures marked NIV are from the *New International Version Study Bible*, copyright © 1985 by the Zondervan Corporation. Used by permission, the Holy Bible, New International Version, copyright © 1973, 1978, 1984 by the International Bible Society.

ISBN: 1-55306-339-2

**For more information or
to order additional copies, please contact:**
Robin Young Goza
401 Thornton Lane
Georgetown, TX 78628 USA
(512) 930-5260

Essence Publishing is a Christian Book Publisher dedicated to furthering the work of Christ through the written word. *Guardian Books* is an imprint of *Essence Publishing*. For more information, contact:
44 Moira Street West, Belleville, Ontario, Canada K8P 1S3.
Phone: 1-800-238-6376. Fax: (613) 962-3055.
E-mail: info@essencegroup.com
Internet: www.essencegroup.com

Printed in Canada
by

Guardian BOOKS

Many thanks to Stephanie and Kimi, my two beautiful daughters, who shared their lives and love with Karen. And to all the doctors, nurses, Child Life specialists, and others who dedicate their lives to helping us with our special needs children.

I would also like to acknowledge Stephanie, Kimi, and my husband Jim, who read the manuscripts numerous times, and also graciously gave up time with their mom and spouse so that I could spend countless hours on the manuscript and its many revisions.

My parents, siblings, and extended family, who have supported me through the walk with Karen, and through birthing this book.

My best friend, Maura Roach, for always "being there."

Emmit Roach, Maura's husband, and a college English teacher, who read my entire manuscript, checking content and grammar.

Linda Hoskins, R.N. and friend, who read the entire manuscript for medical accuracy.

T.E. Allen, M.D.; Carlotta Cagle; Javier Aceves, M.D.; Sally Olsen, R.N.; Richard Andrassy, M.D.; Hugo Caravjal, M.D.; Catherine Young, M.D.; M.K. Thapar, M.D.; James W. Simpson, M.D.; James A. Duff, M.D., P.A.; Chaplain Jack Dugan; Richard Weir, Child Life psychologist; pediatric doctors, nurses and therapists at Brazosport Memorial Hospital, Hermann Hospital, and Driscoll Foundation's Children's Hospital; BACH rehabilitation Center ECI staff; and to all my friends and church family in lake Jackson who helped me with Karen.

Table of Contents

Baby Karen's Gift

I n a world where instant gratification is expected, the accomplishments of a tiny baby who spent much of her life in a hospital or confined to her home may seem insignificant, but those who came into contact with *Baby Karen* (as she was affectionately called by those at our church), found their lives changed, even if only for a short time.

I wish that others could have known Karen as I knew her—her delightful personality, but her definite temper; her complete dependence on us, but her strong desire for independence; her eagerness to be like her sisters, but her strong-willed attempts to be her own person; her fighting spirit, but her need to share her special love with others.

According to many, Karen was a burden, a lot of work. However, like a rose that is cared for properly, with all the proper techniques and nourishment administered lovingly at precise times, she blossomed beautifully and miraculously into someone special, to the amazement of many. She could make us laugh; she could make us cry. We never quite knew what to expect. Like all of God's prize-winning creations, she stirred the hearts of any who ventured near enough to observe her; they would never again be the same. She inspired and affected everyone in such a positive way. However, like all of God's special gifts to mankind (the rose, the rainbow, and many more), they have a beginning and an end. We must enjoy them as intensely as we can while they are here, and then prepare ourselves for His next precious gift.

CHAPTER ONE

No Respecter of Persons

And Peter opened his mouth and said: "most certainly and thoroughly I now perceive and understand that God shows no partiality and is no respecter of persons" (Acts 10:34 Amplified).

We often think that God does special training only for Bible heroes like Moses, Joseph, or Paul, or for well-known evangelists or missionaries. However, one day I realized that God took great care in preparing me for a special task He had for me, too—that of caring for a very special little girl.

When I was a child of about six to nine years old, we lived by some people who had four boys, one of them mentally retarded. His mother had tried to abort him, but he lived, and his mind and body were affected. Unfortunately for him, his home contained very little love and care, so he was often mean. One day while I was playing, he sneaked up behind me and hit me on the back with a stick. Naturally, I cried, and my big brother came out and hit him and chased him home. I remember feeling strangely sorry for the neighbor boy and realizing that he seemed so frustrated because of his disabilities and the way he was treated.

When I was in the sixth grade, we moved to Bellaire, Texas, and lived near a family with five girls. The fourth had Down's syndrome. This little child, however, was born into a loving Christian family and was an affectionate, sweet child. She had her limitations, too, but her family always encouraged her to do whatever she could. I remember my mom telling me that this mother once said that the saddest part about having Kathy was other people's reactions after seeing her. On the playground or at the swimming pool, other mothers would grab up their children and leave as quickly as they could, as if Kathy had some terrible, communicable disease. I remember feeling sad that people would react like that, although I was glad that the mother taught Kathy's sisters not to be angry, but to pity people who didn't know better.

In the neighborhood there was also a boy who was slow in his development. The doctor had been in a hurry when he delivered him and pulled too hard with the forceps, leaving marks on his head for a long time. He, too, had parents who loved him and worked with him, and he had a sweet disposition. I remember at one point he even had a crush on me. I tried to figure out how to stay his friend, but discourage his ideas about my being his girlfriend. I'm sure that Mom helped me, because he and I remained friends until his family moved away.

When I started parochial school in the eighth grade, I met another girl who had physical and mental developmental problems. She had caught a childhood disease from a sibling when she was very young, and it affected her motor control. She was tall for her age, walked a little slowly, and her speech was lethargic and difficult to understand at first. She was about two years behind in school, but her family and the teachers worked with her so she could attain her full potential. By junior high, her development seemed almost normal. She, too, came from a loving family. Love, hard work, and caring had made a significant difference.

In college, I met and dated a man who needed to wear a built-up shoe. At first I hardly noticed his physical handicap, because he seemed to have such a likable personality. He was friendly and liked to tease. Later his true feelings emerged. His dislike for this physical imperfection and his self-pity became obvious. He took me to a party given by his *friends*, walked off and ignored me most of the time, and was rude to me when I asked to be taken home. He insisted that I didn't want to be with him because of his foot, rather than because of his intoxicated and coarse behavior. His jovial nature was just a facade. I wonder what kind of family life he had had.

After a few years in college, I slowly began to move away from the Lord. I gradually listened more to *friends* and worldly ideas than I did to God, family, and my Christian background. Perhaps this backward step caused God to postpone my training for this special assignment. Now, years later, I can only guess.

When I was pregnant with my second daughter, Kimi, I remember wondering if she would have any physical or mental abnormalities, since I was thirty-five years old. The doctor had warned me that pregnant women at that age and beyond have a higher risk factor. I turned back to the Lord in July that year, and Kimi was born in October 1984, healthy and alert.

In December 1986, I lost a baby early in the pregnancy. The doctor called it "empty sac syndrome." Obviously something was wrong with the baby or it wouldn't have stopped growing and simply dissolved or reabsorbed, or whatever it did. It just failed to exist any more. All that was left was a placenta and an *empty sac*.

After the initial shock and hurt, I remember asking the Lord for another child, preferably a boy. I told Him that if I could take care of a baby with problems the way it needed to be done, then that would be okay. If I couldn't, then please give me another normal healthy child, or no child at all. The two girls I had would be enough. (Stephanie is my daughter from a previous marriage.)

Later, a woman with a nineteen-year-old daughter with Down's syndrome joined our church. I remember being drawn to the teenager the first time I saw her. When she sang in the 1988 Christmas program with the adults, I remember crying and praying for her. She marched up front, held her songbook high, and sang her song just like the rest of the adults. However, she seemed more nervous than the rest; she was almost shaking. Then, when the first song or group of songs was over, the childlike part of her nature came out; she curtsied and bowed like a young child would. There was innocence in a grown-up body. Why did I feel such magnetism for this young woman? Why did she pull on my heartstrings?

"There but for the grace of God go I" is an expression that many of us like to say, because it sounds good and it's true. However, most of us don't really grasp its meaning until we are the *there* and not the *I*. I understand it better now, because I have been both.

After the *empty sac,* I thought I would never get pregnant again. When I did, the pregnancy seemed different, but without any obvious complications. The baby wasn't as active, and my tummy wasn't so big and purple the last month that the skin felt as if it couldn't possibly stretch any more. Since the heartbeat sounded okay, the baby's length measured normal for its age on ultrasound, and uterine growth was normal, we felt that maybe *she* was a *he.* That could account for the differences. *He* might just be a little smaller by weight because of my age. Only near the end, when the baby wouldn't move from its breech position and we decided to have it turned, did we suspect anything might be wrong. However, we never expected any serious disabilities.

On December 22, 1988, I began one of the most difficult, and yet rewarding, seasons of my life. God had spent many years preparing me for this important job, and I did my best. He had answered my prayers for another child, and made me realize that we are able to accomplish much more than we think we can. Something we often fail to realize is that God's grace isn't lacking at all with individuals considered by *the world as disabled*. Many times it is poured out in abundance on them; we just often don't see it because of all the difficulties or circumstances.

CHAPTER TWO

A Child is Born

Thursday, December 22, 1988, began as any other near-routine day for an expectant mom whose baby was a week late arriving; my body was not yet ready for the doctor to induce labor. However, the eager anticipation soon turned to apprehension, anguish, anger, and intense fear. A simple stress test to check the baby's reflexes caused the baby's heart rate to drop drastically with each simulated contraction. My obstetrician told me that the baby would probably not be able to survive regular labor contractions, so he could not induce labor or allow me to go into labor on my own. He had to do an emergency Caesarean-section delivery.

I had an epidural, but needed so much medication to keep from feeling the pain—the *knife*—that the doctor explained if the next dose didn't work, they would have to put me out. They didn't want to, since I had recently eaten lunch, and it might make me sick. Finally my abdomen was deadened enough that the doctor started the incisions, but by the time he was making the last few cuts, I definitely felt pressure and *a lot* of discomfort; I could feel each slice, too. I was shaking a lot, from nerves and the cold, and was squeezing my husband's hand as hard as I could.

When the baby arrived at 3:49 p.m., we were all surprised. Not only was *he* a girl, but she was also only 3lbs., 13 oz. (and 17 inches long) and didn't look fully developed; there was skin and bone, but very little fat. Her face looked wrinkled and puffy when they took her to the nursery. The obstetrician panicked; his charts *proved* she was *term*; he was afraid we might think that he had delivered the baby too early. Since my husband Pat was an attorney, he might have even been fearful of a lawsuit.

She was adorable, but so tiny. Why? Why hadn't she gained weight near the end of the pregnancy as my other two girls had? I didn't get to see my baby again until about 9:00 p.m. Her face looked fuller and much prettier then, very feminine, though fragile; she even looked healthy. I got to hold her and try to nurse her, but she was so tiny and so tired that she didn't respond much. I didn't keep her very long, maybe fifteen minutes; I'm not really sure. The nurses said they would bring her every four hours for feeding, so I figured that we would both do better in a few hours. I would not be so sore, and she would be more awake and alert.

I soon realized that something was wrong when the nurses didn't bring her to me every four hours as expected, or at all. When I asked, they told me that they were keeping her in the incubator to take special care of her, because she was so small. Since I was tired and sore from the Cesarean-section delivery, I hadn't argued. I finally walked down to the nursery Friday after lunch. Because she was in the incubator, I could only look at her, not hold or touch her. How I longed to hold her!

Friday night, our pediatrician, Dr. Allen, told me that she was very sick with aspiration pneumonia, and he couldn't promise that she would live. She had amniotic fluid and formula in her lungs and was on antibiotics to keep from getting an infection. Both

Thursday and Friday nights, he had been up at the hospital with her a lot. By then, they needed to send her to Hermann Hospital in Houston, to their neonatal intensive care unit, where they would have the proper-sized respirator and other necessary equipment. He told us that the weather was extremely bad, with fog and rain, and the life flight helicopter might not be able to come. She would probably have to go by ambulance. (Pat had decided to spend the night Friday when we first found out that Karen had problems. I was so glad he was there when the doctor told me that she had to go to Houston.) When I had first found out that my baby was sick Friday, I had called my friend, Aleca, and talked to her. She came to the hospital and told me that her little girl, Stephanie, had had to go to Hermann Hospital because of complications. Although I didn't expect that my baby would need to go, Aleca's words had prepared me for the worst.

I somehow knew that Karen was special when the nurses first brought her to me a few hours after her birth. We hadn't named her yet, because the names that we had picked didn't seem to fit her. I looked through all the names again. Would it be Jennifer Lynn or Cheryl Elizabeth? Neither name seemed right for her then. Jennifer meant *white wave*, and Cheryl was feminine for Charles, which meant *manly*. She was hardly that. I told my husband that we had to have a name for her before they took her to Houston. We finally decided on a name we had considered earlier. Karen means *pure*, and Elizabeth means *God's promise*, or *consecrated to God*. Karen Elizabeth seemed to be a name that fit her and all the circumstances.

Compassionately, Dr. Allen told me that I should go see Karen before they took her to Houston, but I couldn't, not right away; it hurt too much. My stitches hurt from the C-section; my heart hurt from the possible loss and the sure separation. I just seemed to go stiff and could hardly move. I wanted to cry, but that made my abdomen and stitches hurt. My body, especially my feet, seemed really cold. My nerves and the pain would make me shake and feel even colder. I was almost afraid to see her, afraid that it would hurt too much emotionally to see her and know that she would be going and might not come back, even though at the same time I felt that she would be okay and would come back.

Finally, when everyone else was out of the room, I had a *frank* talk with God and told Him just what I thought about the situation. I asked Him what I was supposed to do and other things I don't even remember now—like why little newborn babies have to go through all of this pain and suffering. Like the gentle Father He is, He waited until I was through. Then firmly but gently He spoke to my heart, saying that Karen and my husband needed me in there with her, to visit with her and touch her and talk to her, and that I would just have to quit feeling sorry for myself long enough to help them. Pat came in and out several times during our discussion and I had to keep convincing him that I was okay and just needed time to myself, for *prayer*. I didn't feel like saying that I was fussing at God.

Hesitantly, I made myself go to the special care nursery to see Karen. I was so glad that I did! She was in the incubator, looking so frail. I enjoyed touching her feet and her hands and letting her wrap her tiny fingers around my finger and look at me like she knew who I was and recognized my voice. There seemed to be a special love and trust between us. We took pictures; they might be our only ones. I also asked him to confirm the name for her before they took her to Houston. It was important to me for her to go with a name—Karen Elizabeth.

The doctor, a fine Christian man, suggested that we get her baptized. We had called John, our pastor, earlier about Karen's condition and now asked him to come and dedicate her to God. Dr. Allen allowed him in the special care nursery with us to pray for

Karen's dedication and for us. Then he stayed with us for a while to make sure we were okay. Why did she have to get so sick and leave so soon? It just didn't seem fair. Nothing seemed fair or right at the moment.

When the ambulance attendants arrived with their special incubator, I had to go back to my room. They hooked her up to a respirator and took tests of her blood gases. Her oxygen level was low, as Dr. Allen had suspected. At about 6:00 a.m. on Saturday morning, they brought her to my room so we could see her before she left. After a short time they all left. I felt so empty and helpless!

CHAPTER THREE

My Baby Has What?

On Saturday, December 24, after only a few hours of sleep, my husband left the hospital, went home to eat and clean up, and drove to Hermann Hospital, about an hour away, to see Karen. It was Christmas Eve. I was alone in one hospital; my new baby was alone in another; Daddy was somewhere in between. My oldest daughter, Stephanie, was with her dad in Houston. My four-year-old, Kimi, went with one of my friends, Jana, and her family to Christmas Eve services at their church. Away from all of her family on such a special night, Kimi preferred playing in the nursery with the babies to watching the children's choir sing in the sanctuary. After the service, they brought her to the hospital to see me, until my husband picked her up at 10:00, so she could sleep at home with Daddy on Christmas Eve. It broke my heart, knowing how hard this must have been for her.

Anxious for information, I called the Turner Unit at Hermann and talked to Karen's nurse, Elaine. Karen was ventilated okay and was breathing some on her own. (The ventilator is like a respirator, which helps a person breathe artificially.) An IV was in her scalp and she was on antibiotics, because of the concern that she might have pneumonia. Next, I talked to one of Karen's doctors, who gave me a toll-free number to call in the future. They understood that we needed to save wherever we could.

Sunday, I got a nice Christmas present. The doctor said I could start eating real food, no more liquid diet. I told him that the nurses had asked me so many times if I had passed gas or had a bowel movement that I felt like a toddler whose mom was waiting for her to use the potty for the first time. Since I had cooperated, I thought I had deserved praise or someone should have gotten excited and clapped her hands!

Later that morning, it almost seemed like a real Christmas. My husband brought Kimi and all our presents to the hospital. After opening them, we visited briefly, and then he took Kimi home, with intentions of visiting Karen in the afternoon. He never made it; he was so tired that he took a long nap, until Kimi finally woke him up. It was Christmas!

After the doctor told me I could go home Monday morning, Pat and Kimi came to get me. It was the most empty feeling I had ever experienced, going home from the hospital after having a baby and not taking her with me. To make it worse, she was an hour away, so I couldn't even look at her or hold her before I left. My tummy was still sore, and I didn't feel comfortable making the long drive and then walking all over a big hospital to get to her unit. At twenty-nine, I probably would have gone in a minute; at thirty-nine, I was hesitant. I think I was a little afraid that the stress of the situation would make me cry so hard that I would pop open my stitches. I ached and wanted to cry, but I tried not to because I wanted Kimi to know that I was happy to see her. My friend, Chris, had come over and cleaned the house before I got home, changed the beds, and washed the dishes and clothes. What a blessing!

About noon, I called for a report on Karen. She was off the ventilator, off oxygen, and had good blood gases. (That means the oxygen level was high enough and carbon dioxide was low enough.) They also gave me some startling news:

- Her face was small and unusual.
- They checked her kidneys and heart.
- They did an ultrasound on her abdomen.
- They checked for inherited disease problems.
- They did a karyotype and cultures to check the blood for genetic illness.
- They did a chromosome development, and she seemed to have an extra #18 chromosome, similar to an extra #21 in Down's syndrome.

Fortunately, at the time I didn't grasp what they were saying.

My husband had canceled his plans to get a ride to Houston with some friends, because he thought he needed to stay with me, as well as Kimi. I assured him that I would be fine. When he said that he might go later, I called his sister, Bami. Since he seemed too tired and stressed to drive safely, she agreed to take him to Houston and have her husband and kids watch Kimi and let her spend the night.

On Tuesday when I called Karen's nurse, Lena, I discovered that Karen had already been moved to the Newborn Special Care Nursery, Intermediate Care. One of the doctors called me back later, and said that they would try to bottle feed her that evening and would release her Thursday. We could check Wednesday evening for the time they would be releasing her.

While Pat was running errands later that day, Dr. Hecht, a geneticist, called with some more unusual information about Karen:

- The baby was small.

- Her sutures were overriding.
- Her mouth and nose openings were small.
- She had a receding chin.
- Her ears were low set.
- Her hands were unusual.

She explained that twenty-three chromosomes, or genes, come from Mom and twenty-three from Dad. Sometimes there is an extra #18, which causes a condition called Trisomy 18, or Edward's Syndrome. They had done a chromosome analysis, and the final results would be due Wednesday or Thursday. My husband and I would need to call her office to set up an appointment to speak with her. I really didn't believe her at that point; I wasn't ready to accept what she had to say and did not care to make a special trip to meet her. However, when Pat returned, I told him what she had said. He left for Houston at 7:50 p.m. to see Karen. Mom and Dad arrived at our house shortly after 8:00 p.m., to visit and help. Bami brought Kimi home, asleep, around 9:00. Pat picked up Stephanie from her dad's, and when they got home at 11:00; she was almost asleep. I visited with Mom and Dad for only a short time before we all went to bed. What a horrible, hectic day!

On Wednesday afternoon, Dr. Hecht called again shortly after my husband left for Houston. The preliminary study was complete, and the second study from another harvest was due the next day. Karen definitely had Trisomy 18, three #18 chromosomes in each cell. She also might have a ventricular septal defect (VSD) (a hole between the lower chambers of her heart). Her kidneys looked normal and her brain was structurally normal. These must have been *normal* problems associated with babies with Trisomy 18, a condition they told me occurs in about 0.5 per cent of all live births. We would need to check with the cardiologist or the nursery doctors about her heart condition. We also needed to set up an appointment to discuss the studies with Dr. Hecht the following week. She would send us a book written to help families understand and cope with Trisomy 18. Reality was beginning to sink in.

She also told me over the phone about one case study on Trisomy 18, done in Australia, which included 48 cases:

- Five were detected with amniotic fluid tests and eliminated.
- Forty-three cases remained.
- Seventy per cent died by one month.
- Fourteen per cent of those left died by the first year.
- Of those, most lived 100 to 1000 days, a maximum of about three years.
- Most who lived longer had no heart abnormality.

The resulting statistics indicated:

- Many babies die soon after birth.
- They have a decreased life span the first year, a significantly shortened life span in general.
- Most who live longer have no heart abnormality.
- Survivors have delayed milestones, which could be significant.

After I told my parents, I called our pastor to tell him what Dr. Hecht had said. Then I called Bami to tell her. Pat stopped at Bami's on the way home from Houston, and she talked with him.

Later, I called and talked to Karen's nurse, Shirley. Karen would be leaving Houston between 8:00 and 9:00 a.m. on Thursday and arriving at the hospital in Lake Jackson by 10:00. They were feeding her then by tube only, discontinuing the oral feeding.

On Thursday my husband had to go back to work. Karen left Houston at 8:30 and got back to Brazosport Memorial Hospital at

10:00 a.m. as planned. Unfortunately, Mom, Dad, the girls, and I were not dressed and ready to go to the hospital until about noon. When we got there, Karen had an IV in her head and a tube in her mouth for feeding. Her check-in weight was 4lbs., 1oz. Mom and Dad and I got to take turns holding her, two at a time in the special care nursery. The girls watched us awhile through the windows and watched TV in the waiting room, too. I could hardly believe that I was finally allowed to hold her again; it felt so good.

On Friday, we needed to take care of other business before seeing Karen. First we got Kimi's stitches out of her nose. On December 20, Bami's dog, Midnight, had bit Kimi's nose and scratched the corner of her eye, when they had kept the girls while we went to a party. Dr. Allen was on call, met us at his office at 10:45 p.m., and put four stitches in Kimi's nose. At the party, Mary Henderson had given me fifty dollars and told me that the Lord had told her to give it to me, but I didn't look at the amount until later. I had a ten-dollar bill and a one-dollar bill in my purse already, and the cost for Kimi's stitches was sixty dollars. It must have been God! Next, Dad, Kimi, and I took Karen's birth announcement baby ring to the florist to have them replace *Baby Girl Taylor* with her name. Then our family went to see Karen at about noon, while Dad and Mom stayed and began fixing our washing machine, stereo, and sewing machine.

Although they had originally planned to stay much longer, Mom and Dad suddenly decided to leave Saturday at 5:30 p.m. to go to Houston to spend New Year's Eve with Grandma Lucy. I knew that Mom's explanation for their sudden change of plans did not seem right, but only much later did I find out that Dad had told Mom to get packed and ready to leave. He had reached his limit of seeing Pat watch television and read while they did all the repairs, cleaned the house, fixed the meals, and took care of the children. Pat did not know what to do to help, and Dad is not good at delegating work when he does repairs, or asking for help when he needs is working. He merely *expected* the offer. Perhaps Pat should have continued to offer to do what he could, in terms of cleaning the house and watching the kids. Since he had gone for days with little sleep, and had started back to work Thursday, he probably thought it was a deserved break. They obviously didn't have the same manual of unwritten male rules. Mom finished as much as she could before they left, and made up the story of needing to be with Grandmother to keep from hurting my feelings.

That evening, our family went to see Karen. One of the nurses, Deb, had her party hat on, ready to celebrate in the nursery with the babies. She was so easy to talk to; we mostly talked about doctors and children. When we got home, I didn't feel a lot like celebrating New Year's Eve, but I knew we should for the girls. We had eggnog, cokes, and popcorn and played games and enjoyed each other's company. Then we watched television when it got close to midnight, so we could celebrate as the New Year arrived.

For several more weeks, I went to see Karen every day either during the afternoon or in the evening, or occasionally both, for about one to two hours at a time. My husband and the girls would get bored and go watch TV. I would rock Karen and give her a small bottle. The girls couldn't usually come into the special care nursery with her, but a few times they were allowed to go into one of the labor rooms and put on a hospital gown, wash their hands, and wear a mask if they had the sniffles. Then they, too, could hold and rock Karen. Stephanie would get upset and cry if Pat got overly protective and made her position her mask just right, or made her rewash her hands every time she touched her face or her mask. The mask was too big and would hurt her eyes or her neck, causing her to reach up and adjust it. She would finally tell us to forget about letting her hold the baby, that she would eventually hold Karen later. He got so nervous about having the girls do everything just right because he didn't want Karen to get any germs. Perhaps he got carried away by the elaborate setup and scrubbing procedure, and became overly cautious. However, we needed to allow them to enjoy her in a more relaxed manner. Although Karen did need to be protected, she also needed to be loved by her sisters as well as her parents. It hurt me to see them feel left out, or even excluded.

On January 22, 1989, I made a one-month birthday cake for Karen and took it to the nursery for the nurses to share. Since most Trisomy 18 babies did not live past their first month, this was a good reason to celebrate and take pictures. The nurses loved it—not only the cake, but also the reason for it. I made another cake for both Stephanie and Karen for us to enjoy at home. (Stephanie's birthday was January 21.) Bami and her children came over to help us celebrate, although Stephanie had already had a skating birthday party the day before. Since it was at the skating rink, I didn't have to clean house and make a lot of plans, and she probably enjoyed it more anyway. Time and energy were often scarce then.

When Karen was about five weeks old, Dr. Allen told us that she was finally almost big enough to be released. She should weigh 5lbs., but she was 4lbs. and 12 or 13 ounces. We met with him in his office after hours, and he explained to us our three basic options for her release. We could go to Hermann Hospital and have a gastrostomy feeding tube put directly into her stomach; we could learn how to tube feed her; or our third option he realized was not really an option for us. He began to cry as he told us that our last option was to take her home and try to feed her by mouth and watch her slowly die. We agreed to take her to Houston and abide by the decisions of those doctors regarding the first two choices. We asked our church for prayer for wisdom for the doctors and for us to know how to feed Karen. We also asked for continued prayer for her sucking and swallowing coordination and for weight gain. In addition, we prayed that she would not be retarded and would someday have only two #18 chromosomes. I didn't think it would hurt to ask big!

On Friday, 1989, Pat and I checked Karen out of the hospital in Lake Jackson and took her straight to see Dr. Aceves and his assistant, Sally Olsen, in Houston at the medical clinic for the University of Texas. He examined her and advised us to learn to insert a tube into her nose to feed her, so she could still practice taking a bottle. At that time, he felt she was too little to risk surgery for a gastrostomy, because they used a general anesthetic. We both took her to Hermann Hospital and learned how to insert the tube into her nose. The diameter of the 8 FR (French) tube was too large for her nose, so we used a 5 FR tube, but it was so narrow that we had to get one long enough for gravity to help get the formula through it a little faster. When we were learning to insert it, the tube would sometimes come out her other nostril or even the same nostril we inserted it in or would get tangled up at the back of her throat. I would get so upset hearing her cry or scream that it would make me cry, too. Finally I asked God what we should do. This was too upsetting, but I knew we had to be able to feed her. He reminded me early Saturday morning of His promise (not audibly, of course), *I will never leave you nor forsake you* (Heb. 13:5 KJV). I didn't know what He meant at the time, but it calmed me down long enough for me to get a little sleep. Later that night He told me to learn how to insert the tube through her mouth too, as an alternative. We learned how to do that Sunday and then left late Sunday afternoon. God is helpful, just like a daddy, if we calm down long enough to listen to Him and take His advice.

Grandma Lucy had come earlier Sunday to visit and hold Karen. They both loved it. Grandma sang to her, naturally. (At one time she sang in her church choir, the Houston Chorale, and a ladies' singing group, but finally cut back to just the church choir, and finally to none.)

It seemed so strange to finally have Karen at home. Kimi was staying at Bami's and Stephanie was at her daddy's. It was quiet, except for the crying of a baby.

Because of her Trisomy 18, Karen had become a statistic to many doctors and nurses. Most Trisomy 18's who are born do not live past the first month or two; they don't have muscle tone; they are severely mentally retarded; few make it to one year; and they can't do much of anything but lie there and take up space. Karen proved them wrong. She was not a statistic, but a real live baby, and she taught a lot of doctors and nurses some invaluable lessons.

CHAPTER FOUR

An Angel, or Angels?

Be not forgetful to entertain strangers: for thereby some have entertained angels unawares (Heb. 13:2 KJV).

For as long as I can remember, Karen liked to lie down on my pillow and look around the room. At first I thought that when she seemed to stare for a long time in one direction, she was staring at an object or shadows or light reflections on the wall or ceiling. Later I realized that she would frequently stare at the ceiling where there were no shadows or light patterns or objects. I began to wonder if she could perhaps see or hear something that I couldn't, because she would sometimes change her facial expressions, smiling or whatever, as if seeing and hearing something. I told a few other women what she did, and all of them seemed to agree. Although we did not all belong to the same church and had different religious backgrounds, all said the same thing that I had thought, "She's looking at angels."

After reading *Angel Unaware*, by Dale Evans Rogers, I wondered if Karen was really an angel sent by God or just a very special baby who was very sensitive to the spiritual world. In particular, I noticed that she would get well quickly when we prayed or called the prayer chain to pray for her. In contrast, it seemed that she would become ill again or her fever would go up quickly whenever there was discord in the home.

On March 23, Karen had her three-month checkup. She weighed 6lbs., 9 oz., not a good weight for a three-month-old baby, but great for Karen. One of the symptoms of her chromosome problem was a condition called *failure to thrive*, which meant she didn't gain weight easily, no matter how much food she *ate*. As Dr. Allen was asking if her seeing and hearing were good, she was looking at the Holly Hobbie print on the wallpaper of his office. If she didn't see the different colors in the print, she wouldn't have looked around at it so much. There were no other pictures or things hanging on the wall to get her attention. She also looked at people, shiny objects, and her stuffed toys. She didn't much like her toys, though, and usually threw them out of her car seat. A few days before, she had stroked her small stuffed lamb, however, and acted like she was trying to pull lint off of it, because she liked to grab lint and keep it in her fist.

As for her hearing, she knew the sound of different people's voices, especially Mommy's. She also liked music. Whenever I rocked her, she liked me to play the praise tapes Mike Smith had given us. When a tape was over and I didn't get up and change it within a few minutes, she usually started fussing. After the music started, she would calm down again.

On March 31, Karen went in for an examination of her ears. During the morning, she had been rubbing against her left ear and left cheek with her pointer finger, while fussing and snorting because of congestion I could not clear out even with nose drops and the bulb syringe. Dr. Allen said that her ear canals were so small that he couldn't even see into her inner ear to see if there was an infection. Since there was no fever, he didn't want to treat her with medication yet. We would have to wait and watch. By then she was 6lbs., 15oz.

Karen had started moving her head over to the edge of her car seat and hanging it off the sponge inner pad, which was for small babies. When she lay on her tummy, she would pick up her head and turn it from one side to the other. Those may not have been big deals for other babies her age, but for her, they were major accomplishments.

She loved moving her tongue around inside her mouth and outside her mouth, like sticking it out and making funny faces with it. She also liked to blow bubbles (her saliva) from her mouth. That really seemed fun to Karen.

When it was dark and she lay on her side on the pillow beside me, if I moved away so she was not touching my arm or face with her hands, she reached out looking for me, sometimes whacking me in the face. If she didn't feel me, she would *nose dive* with the top of her head toward me, bending at the waist, until her head or hands touched me. It was comical watching her.

During the last week in March, her nose was so congested that she would wake up fussy, and if I did not do something quickly, she would poke me in the face with one or both hands and then snort with her nose, or cry and then snort, as if trying to tell me to clear her nose—now!

While rocking Karen, I had caught up on a lot of reading that had been sitting there for over a year—Kenneth Hagin's magazines, *Word of Faith*; many of his small booklets and books; and a lot of newsletters from other ministries. It was interesting, informative, and encouraging. Around the first of April, I felt that the Lord was telling me that if I would have Kenneth Hagin lay hands on Karen and pray for her, He would heal her. I got so excited that I couldn't wait to figure out how we could get her to Tulsa, Oklahoma, where Hagin was. I was almost certain that I wouldn't be going there any time soon. I wondered if Sandy Taylor (our youth pastor's wife who is an R.N.) would like to take her the next time she and Craig went to Rhema in Tulsa for another seminar. I didn't really think so, since she would have to feed Karen every three hours around the clock. I figured that we would have to wait until Rev. Hagin would come closer to Lake Jackson.

I told my husband about Hagin, and he halfheartedly said, "Okay." A few days later, he came to me with a funny look on his face and said, "You'll never believe this, but Hagin is going to be at Lakewood Church in Houston in the middle of April." That was a confirmation to me of what I had heard in my heart.

I called our pastor, John Haynes, to see if he thought it would be possible for us to see Hagin individually, since Karen was not supposed to be in crowds. (Dr. Allen advised us not to have her around a lot of people, especially children, because her immune system was not fully developed.) John said it would be worth a try to call and gave me Jim Graff's number at Lakewood. He was an associate pastor who had been a visitor at our church several times. His wife, Tamara (John Osteen's daughter), had been at our church for some of the ladies' meetings, too. Graff's secretary told me that he said they could not make promises for a visiting pastor's time. She suggested that I call Hagin's personal secretary. When I called her, she was sympathetic, but said that if he did that for one person, it would set a precedent and he would have to do it for others. I told her that I was sure God wanted Kenneth Hagin to lay hands on her, and if God could heal her, He could also protect her in crowds. I called Sandy Taylor, since she was a nurse and a Christian, to see if that made sense, or sounded Okay, from a medical standpoint as well as a spiritual standpoint. She agreed that God would take care of Karen if He were telling me to do it to heal her. The next morning Renee, Osteen's secretary, called to tell me that they had heard about my baby and that John Osteen (the pastor at

Lakewood) said to bring Karen about ten minutes before 7:00 p.m. on Sunday, April 16, the night Hagin would be talking on healing. I could hardly believe it, but I knew it had to be God! I was so ecstatic that I called John Haynes and Sandy. I thought that that would be the greatest birthday gift I could get (April 17)—the complete healing of my daughter!

John got us a special valet parking pass for Sunday night and gave us instructions on how to get there. He also suggested that my husband make a trial run to the church, since he had to go to Houston for business anyway. He even encouraged us to get there between 5:30 and 6:00 p.m. because of parking. So many cars would be backed up on that street waiting to get into the parking area that we wouldn't want to take a chance on being late.

That weekend, Stephanie went to her daddy's and we took Kimi to Bami's. We left later than we planned, but arrived at Lakewood Church before 6:00 p.m. We fed Karen in the car and then took her in at about 6:30. They had told us that if we got there at 6:30 or later, we would be able to go into Osteen's personal office. We just needed to ask for Osteen's personal bodyguard, Jesse, who would be waiting for us. Unfortunately, right before we went in, a car had hit a lady and an officer as they both crossed the street to go to the church. Some young man's brakes had failed. As we went across the street, the woman was still lying there, unable to get up, and people were standing around her praying until the ambulance could arrive. Since Jesse had to be outside taking care of that situation, he wasn't able to meet us. Finally, someone told us to go upstairs and sit on one of the couches off to the side. Right before 7:00 they told us to go down to the office, because Rev. Hagin was ready for us.

Rev. and Mrs. Hagin were waiting for us and asked us if this was the baby. Pat was holding her in her car seat. Rev. and Mrs. Hagin laid hands on her and started praying for her right away. He prayed that she be completely healed in her whole body from the top of her head to her toes. That too confirmed to me that God had arranged the whole thing, because I was sure that He had told me that she would be *completely* healed—everything! Hagin doesn't normally pray for someone if he feels that God says, "No." When he was through praying, he told us to thank and praise God for her healing. All I could do was cry and thank God and Rev. Hagin.

Donna (one of the ladies from our church) had helped get us to the right places when we got to Lakewood. She went into the room with us when Hagin prayed and later said that she felt the power of God in the room. She also reminded me of what Hagin had said, "Remember, God's healing power went right into that baby. Don't accept anything that the devil tries to put on her." All I could remember was what he had told us about praising and thanking God and that God's healing power had gone right into her body.

Unfortunately, on Monday, April 17, Karen woke up with the first fever over 100° that she ever had. Carlotta, Dr. Allen's daughter and office manager, said it could be just a cold and not to worry unless her temperature went up more or her sinuses looked infected. She then suggested that I get some infant Tylenol. On Wednesday (Dr. Allen's day off), Karen's fever went up more, so I took her to Dr. Imperial. She knew of Karen and had seen her a few months before at the hospital. She also told me that the letter about Karen and abortion, which I had written to the Facts newspaper (see appendix), was posted in the nursery at the hospital. Karen had a sinus infection and bronchiolitis. (I had gotten concerned when the stuffiness went from her nose to her throat and then to her chest.) She took Amoxil antibiotic, and was finally back to normal in about two weeks. Unfortunately, it took her longer than most babies to get over an infection, because of her inadequate immune system.

We continued to believe that our prayers were being answered, in spite of all the circumstances. We had hoped for an instant miracle, but realized that God always answers in His time and in His way. I felt that our trip to Houston was not wasted effort, but was an act of obedience and a sign of our faith. (I saw the movie, *Rudy*, later, where Rudy said, "We pray on our time; God answers on his time.")

On May 1, Karen learned to smile, or more correctly, to grin— a funny toothless grin. She had been watching Kimi talk, laugh, and giggle on their dad's side of the bed. She was lying on my pillow during or after a feeding. All of a sudden she gave a big grin. When she got such a good response from us, she did it over and over—at least half a dozen times. We hugged and kissed her and told her how cute she was. She loved it! She grinned for Stephanie, too, when she got home from school and for Pat when he got home from work. It just took a little coaxing.

On Friday, May 5, Karen went for a well-baby checkup at 4 months. She got her first immunization shots, DTP, and her oral polio vaccine. Naturally, she got fussy right away. They gave her some infant Tylenol and told me to give it to her every four hours as long as she fussed. We could finally quit giving it to her on Sunday evening. While she was lying on my pillow for her feeding, Karen learned how to throw her first temper tantrum. She kicked her leg back against the bed and yelled, "Eh!" at the same time. Then she kicked her leg back and hit her arm back against the bed and went, "Eh!" She did this several times. It was so funny to watch. She felt bad; she did not like it; and she wanted everyone to know. This was a month for firsts, from grins to tantrums!

On Thursday, May 18, Karen got another upper respiratory infection and was running a fever of about 99° to 101°. This time I took her to Dr. Allen. He put her on Ceclor (an antibiotic), Triaminic infant drops (an antihistamine), and Tylenol, as needed.

Her fever would go away in a day or less, but then come back two or three days later. After a week of this, I took her back on Thursday, May 25. Dr. Allen said to finish the antibiotic, but stop the Triaminic and Tylenol, unless the fever was 102° or higher, to give her body a chance to fight it. She finished her Ceclor on Saturday and was fine all weekend. On Tuesday her fever started again and went between 100° and 101.7° off and on. Wednesday evening I went to church. When I came back, she felt hotter than usual. Her fever was 103°. I gave her Tylenol, and it went down to 102.5°. My husband told me to get some sleep, that he would feed her and keep up with her temperature. Grateful, I closed the door to the extra bedroom and crawled into bed, ready to get a few hours of much-needed sleep.

CHAPTER FIVE

Not Hermann Again!

At 6:00 a.m. on Thursday, June 1, I woke up and felt a compelling urge to go check on Karen. I had been sleeping in the extra bedroom; Pat and Karen had been in our bed. As I entered the room, she was crying strangely and her breathing was odd, too, kind of deep. When I touched her, she felt **really** hot. I tried to wake him up and ask him why he had not heard her cry. Half asleep, he looked at me quizzically and asked, "What?" When I asked again, he took the earplugs out of his ears. I was horrified! He explained that he used them because her whimpering kept him awake and there was nothing he could do anyway to make her feel better or quit crying. (Since she choked easily, even on the mucus that drained down her throat, I always tried to sleep beside her to hear her.) He then told me that he had fed her at 3:00 a.m. and, since her fever was only 101°, he went back to bed and fell asleep near 4:00 a.m. I promised myself never again to ask him to watch her at night.

Since her fever was 105.8° by the time I went to the bedroom that morning, I called the hospital to see if I should bring her in. They told me to call her doctor-on-call first. Dr. Imperial told me that all they would do at the hospital to get her fever down was to put her in a tub or sink full of water, so I should try that. I put her in the sink with lukewarm water, and her fever went down to about 104°. Over the next two hours, her fever went up and down from about 101° or 102° to 105° and more. At 8:20 a.m. I called Carlotta at home, told her about the fever variations, and asked her if she thought her dad, Dr. Allen, would want to see Karen. She was sure he would and told me to bring her in by 9:15, before most of the other patients would be there.

By then Pat had taken my car to the Chrysler dealer in Angleton to have it repaired. Why did he need to take my car that day, when Karen was so sick? If I needed to take her to the doctor, I would then need to drive his car. I thought he knew I didn't like driving his car, since it was standard shift rather than automatic. I didn't drive standard, at least not well. Unfortunately, I had been too busy earlier trying to contact her doctors and reduce her fever to argue with him and insist on keeping my car. Since his sister, Bami, lived in Angleton, I called her to see if she could bring him home to drive his car. She checked at the Chrysler dealer and discovered that he could bring the car home, because they couldn't work it into their schedule that day. Why hadn't he called them first to check? I felt like I was about to go crazy. Luckily, Bami said that she would take us to the doctor and keep Kimi, so that her brother could go to work. We arrived at the doctor's at 9:20, and Dr. Allen informed me quickly that Karen's lungs sounded like pneumonia. We needed to take her straight to the emergency room at the hospital, and he would meet us there as soon as possible. At the hospital, they checked her blood gases and other things and decided that she needed to be ventilated and have more extensive tests. Meanwhile, I had to wait in the lobby.

Finally someone came out to the waiting room and told me that she would need to be life-flighted to Hermann Hospital. "No," I thought, "not Hermann again!" That was the first time I cried, when I called my husband to tell him and called Claire, our pastor's wife, to tell her. Our pastor, John, got there a minute or two later. I cried trying to tell him the details. John got his daughter to bring him some cash so that he could give us $200 to help with hospital expenses—food, parking, and whatever—and told us not to pay him back or worry about tithing on it. (He knew that Pat tried to make sure that we tithed on every gift that came into our household, as well as on his paychecks.)

At 12:30 p.m. Karen left in the Life Flight helicopter, with her nurse, Mitzi, and her paramedic, Scott. Pat and I rushed there in our car as fast as we could. I was thankful that I didn't have to drive. When we arrived, Karen was ventilated with 100% oxygen. By 10:00 p.m., the air in her ventilator was reduced to only 82% oxygen. Her respirations were set to fifteen per minute on the machine; while on her own she could do fifteen to thirty respirations per minute. What a horrible way to start the summer!

The next days and weeks were filled with questions, numbers, percentages, tests, diagnoses, more tests, new diagnoses, and lots of spare time to read, write my thoughts about what was happening, take notes on what the doctors told me, talk to other parents in the lobby of pediatrics intensive care, or just stare into space and go numb or ask the rhetorical question, "Why?"

We had let Stephanie finish her last day of school and attend the end of the year party, rather that pulling her out of school, and made arrangements for her to go home with neighbors, who would tell her what happened. When we got home that first night, we arranged for someone to watch the girls while I was at the hospital and my husband at work. On June 2, I arrived at the hospital before 1:00 p.m., ready to spend that night, and as many as it took, to get Karen home again.

The doctor in charge of the Pediatric Critical Care Unit (PCCU) gave me some data about Karen later that day:

- Her weight at 2:30 p.m. was 8 lb. 8 oz.
- At the same time her fever was 102°F.
- She had pneumonia, mostly in the right lung, some in the left.
- Karen had a large ventricular septal defect (VSD) (a hole in the lower chambers of the heart) and an enlarged heart.

Karen had probably had a seizure when she first got there. They did an EEG on her brain to verify their diagnosis, but the results would not be back until Monday. (They said she had had a seizure because her eyes rolled back in her head and she smacked her lips a lot, but I told them that her eyes had done that since she was born. Besides, she was dehydrated and thirsty and did not do as much sucking as most babies, so her attempts at sucking probably sounded like smacking. Dr. Allen even laughed when I told him what they said about her eyes and the seizure and said, "They've always done that.") They would do a blood transfusion at about 6:00 or 8:00 p.m. They would try to take out the oxygen tube later that night.

- Some of the statistics I recorded that Friday were:
- 1:00 p.m.: 52% oxygen, 5.19 respirations by machine, 38 to 42 on her own
- 1:30 p.m.: back up to 60% oxygen
- 5:20 p.m.: 50% oxygen, 10.2 respirations by machine
- 8:30 p.m.: 40% oxygen, 10 respirations by machine
- 10:30 p.m.: 40% oxygen, 5 respirations by machine

The respiratory therapists kept changing the percentage of oxygen, which she received in the air from the ventilator. They also changed the amount of respirations the machine would do for her. I didn't really understand it all, but I realized that when those numbers got low enough, her own breathing was good enough for them to take her off of the machine.

- 11:30 p.m.: They suctioned Karen to get ready to take out the tube and to disconnect the ventilator.
- 12:00 midnight: The tube is out. She is off the ventilator. Her head is under an oxygen hood. She's free again!

Unfortunately, because they needed to retape her IV at 12:30 a.m. and she went to sleep immediately afterwards, I did not get to hold her that night. I went to bed feeling sad and empty. Between 10:00 and 11:00 a.m. the next day, I finally got to hold Karen. By 4:00 p.m. the oxygen level in the hood was down to 55%, and her own respirations were normal at forty to fifty per minute. The rest of Saturday and Sunday must have been a blur to me, for I recorded nothing else.

On Monday, June 5, I talked with Dr. Aceves, who explained that Karen had had heart failure when she first arrived. I had seen his nurse, Sally Olsen, earlier that day and had given her a small picture of Karen and a copy of the newspaper article I had written about Karen and abortion. I really liked Dr. Aceves and Sally. They seemed like warm-hearted people who honestly cared about their patients and treated them as individuals, not statistics.

On Tuesday morning, June 6, they took Karen out from under the oxygen hood and replaced it with a nasal cannula (two tubes containing oxygen going into her nose). When the oxygen from the hood had been reduced to 35%, the oxygen saturation in her blood (SATS) remained at 95%, almost perfect. They weaned her from the ventilator to the hood to the cannula and hopefully to no assistance later. Their aim was, as always, to have her breathe on her own as much and as quickly as possible.

Later that day, the doctors explained that Karen's tests had shown no seizures. (We had tried to tell them!) Instead, they decided that the problem had been heart failure, which Dr. Aceves had briefly mentioned to me on Monday. Her kidney was slightly enlarged and the enzyme level had been up, but was normal at that time. (Measuring enzyme levels in the blood can be useful for diagnosing disorders of certain organs or tissues.)[1] They thought that she might have had hyaline membrane disease when she was a newborn, because patches were on her lungs. They also thought that she might have had chronic aspirations. (I recently checked Karen's records from December 24 through December 29, 1988, when she was at Hermann Hospital as a newborn. One R.N. noted, "Eyes roll upward." So much for the seizure! Records also included, "The patient noticed to have aspirated with respiratory distress on day of life 1." Comments included with an x-ray on December 24 included, "The chest shows severe hyaline membrane disease." On the next day they said, "The lungs are quite hazy. These findings are compatible with hyaline membrane disease." It seemed odd to me that it would have taken them so long to diagnose what doctors and nurses had already recorded at the same hospital almost six months earlier. I do realize, however, that medicine is not an exact science, and they were probably eliminating other things first.)

They had even done a lumbar puncture test to check Karen for bacterial meningitis, but no bacteria were evident in her spinal fluid. (Meningitis is an inflammation of the membranes of the spinal cord or brain, caused by bacteria, viruses, or other organisms, which reach the membranes through the blood or lymph or adjacent body structures. Bacterial meningitis is life threatening and needs prompt treatment. Its main symptoms, which can develop rapidly, sometimes over a few hours, are fever, severe headache, nausea and vomiting, dislike of light, and a stiff neck, and are followed by drowsiness and sometimes loss of consciousness.

Meningococcal meningitis, the most common form of bacterial meningitis, probably affects between 2,000 and 5,000 young people—70 per cent under the age of five—in the United States each year.)[2] They had inserted a hollow needle into the lower part of her spinal canal between two lumbar vertebrae to withdraw and examine cerebrospinal fluid from her spinal cord. They checked and found no bacterial infection in her lungs either, except on the ventilator tube, but it would not have caused meningitis. All of that sounded like it hurt.

They prepared to do a barium swallow test the next day to see how well Karen swallowed, to check the sucking reflex and coordination of sucking and swallowing, and to see whether the liquid went down her esophagus or into her nose or lungs. By looking under fluorescent lighting to watch the barium, they would also check to see if there was a hole or connection between her esophagus and trachea so that food was going into her lungs when she ate or spit up. Some of the junk they suctioned out of her lungs could have been in there for a long time.

Karen would be ready after the test the next day to go to a room on the general pediatrics floor, where Dr. Aceves would be her primary physician. Her cardiologist would be Dr. Thapar. Additionally, she could have gastrostomy surgery some time after the tests, so that a feeding tube could be placed directly into her stomach. We would no longer have to put tubes through her nose or mouth, irritating her nose and throat, and giving her great pleasure when she caught us off guard and quickly pulled them out.

On Wednesday, June 7, they did the barium test. She got 80cc. of barium between 10:00 a.m. and 12:30 p.m. and 70cc. of formula with potassium and sodium chloride by 12:45 p.m. Since they were ready to send her to a room at 3:00 p.m., she also got her 3:00 p.m. feeding at 2:45 p.m. That was a **lot** of food for one little tummy!

By 1:45 p.m. two neurologists came into the room to check Karen and ask questions. The more experienced one suggested that she should have a brain scan to see if there was damage anywhere on her brain, for future reference. He also asked me if my husband or I had had chromosome tests after Karen did. I said, "No." Just as he opened her diaper to check her there (What that part of her anatomy had to do with her brain, I have yet to figure out!), she started having a bowel movement (b.m.). I hadn't noticed the b.m. at first and had told them that while her diaper was open, I would like to change it, since I had noticed earlier that it was wet. He condescendingly remarked that I sure did need to change it, because it was starting to smell bad. (Actually, I think he raised his eyebrows, frowned, and sourly said, "Pleeeease do!") She had to relieve herself of so much barium and formula that she soiled three diapers before she finished, two while the doctors were there (or at least the more experienced one, because the other one left earlier, when they first saw the messy diaper). After I put the first two diapers on her, I told him that I would just close it up and change her later and let him finish his exam. I could hardly keep from exploding with laughter.

Karen had perfect timing. The doctors seemed so clinical and aloof. She brought them down to earth quickly. I agreed with her feelings (or whatever you would call it) about the doctors. God has to have a sense of humor!

CHAPTER SIX

Surgery, Stress, Insensitivity, and Swelling

At 4:00 p.m. on Wednesday, June 7, one of the assistant pediatric surgeons came into the room. After checking with the cardiologist and others, they had tentatively planned Karen's gastrostomy surgery for early Friday morning. Another assistant came in later to examine Karen and to have me sign papers. That evening a nurse told me that surgery would be Thursday morning between 8:00 a.m. and noon. I was beginning to get used to their *decisiveness*. Actually, someone finally came to take Karen to surgery at 5:30 p.m. on Thursday, June 8. They had changed plans again! (I realized that emergencies always needed to take precedence over elective surgeries, but so many changes were wearisome to anxious parents, at least to me.) The man got her charts and things together and hooked her up to a portable oxygen container. I followed as he took her down to the operating room's holding room, and we were there about thirty minutes. It was so cold in the room that I was afraid Karen would get sick if she stayed there much longer. When the doctors were finally ready at almost 6:30 p.m., I went back to the lobby to wait.

One of the assistants had said that surgery should take about two hours and to go to her room and wait there for them to call me.

Later I told one of the nurses at the nurses' station that I would be in the lobby waiting for my family. When my husband and daughters arrived, we visited in the lobby for a while and then went to the playground directly outside the lobby. I cautiously went back to Karen's room before 8:00 p.m., in case the doctors called early. At 8:30 p.m., a nurse came into the room and told me that I would need to clear out my stuff. Bewildered, I told her that I was waiting for a call about Karen. She checked and found out that someone had called the nurse's station at 7:30 p.m. to tell them Karen would not be returning to her room, and she was taken to PCCU near 8:00 p.m. I was so frustrated that no one had even bothered to tell me where she was when she came out of surgery, so that I could be with her as quickly as possible while she recovered!

At 9:45 p.m. I was still waiting to see Karen. The rest of my family had left between 9:15 and 9:30 p.m. The doctors and nurses were cleaning her up and checking the placement of her ventilator tube. They were supposed to tell me when she was ready, but I was afraid that they would forget that, too. I called the PCCU nurses again and finally got in at 9:55 p.m., almost two hours after she had arrived. By then I was starting to cry.

Karen's nurse, Sherri, apologized for the delay and explained that Karen's first ventilator tube had not been put in far enough and they had tried to reposition it. Unfortunately, Karen managed to use her tongue and push it out while it was untaped, and they had for a brief moment glanced the other way to get something. Additionally, because of her pain medication (and her stubbornness), Karen would not take a breath on her own, to avoid the need for replacement of the ventilator. Dr. Young later said that it seemed like Karen just stared at her and refused to take a breath. Because the first tube had come out and Karen wouldn't breathe, they had to put another tube down her throat as quickly as possible. That made her throat swell even more, so they gave her some steroids to make the swelling go down. Instead of being able to take her off the ventilator that night like they had planned, they had to wait until the next day.

While the surgeons were implanting the gastrostomy tube, they discovered that Karen's gut was twisted and corrected the kink to avoid problems later. They also removed membrane, which was connecting her umbilical area to her gut and verified that there were no gastric fluids remaining, which could cause ulcers later. All of this was in addition to the planned gastrostomy and Nissen fundoplication (wrapping part of the top of the stomach around the esophagus so that food would go in, but would have a harder time going back up and out).

Thursday morning before the surgery, Sally had introduced me to Brenda Ross and two of her five children. Brandi was two in March and had Trisomy 13; Niki was the oldest. Brandi had a cleft palate and no ears, although she did have at least part of her inner ears and could hear with a hearing aid. They were planning surgery later to correct part of the problem. Brenda and I talked for quite a while and seemed to have a lot in common. It was so helpful to talk with another mother who had a child with a similar condition, deeply loved her daughter, and had a strong desire to do whatever it would take to help her daughter reach her full potential.

On Friday, I finally woke up enough to get out of bed at 9:40 a.m. I quickly brushed my teeth and hair and went into PCCU to see Karen before the doctors' rounds at 10:00. She opened her eyes and tried to move, but her arms were pinned down to prevent her from pulling out the tube to the ventilator. She squirmed and cried, but made no noise because of the tube in her throat. Because of her swollen trachea, the doctors thought they might need to wait another day to remove the ventilator tube. I left to clean up and eat lunch and returned at 12:30 p.m. As I walked into Karen's room, I could hear her faintly crying. That meant her swelling was going down! They pulled out her ventilator tube at approximately 3:00 p.m. Although I had to leave for that, I came back at 4:00 p.m. While I was in the lobby waiting, Sally Olsen brought me some trisomy information, which my husband had requested. When I returned, I finally got to hold Karen and rock her for about one hour, from 4:30 to 5:30. It was wonderful!

Pat would have liked the nurse that Karen had that day. She came in to take blood from Karen's arm to check her SATs (saturation of oxygen level in the blood). Because she had thought it might take as long as 30 minutes, when she drew blood the first try, she was excited and exclaimed, "Praise the Lord!" Few people are willing to give credit where it is due, especially at work.

At 4:00 p.m. one of the assistant surgeons came in to explain in more detail what had happened in the surgery. Karen's large intestine had been twisted around and held in the wrong place by some connective tissue. When they cut the tissue, the intestines fell into the right place. She also had a Meckel diverticulum, a growth similar to an appendix, but on the small intestine. Since it was broad-based (wide at the part that connected to the intestine), they left it alone (did not try to cut it off), because it would not be likely to get infected, as it would if it were narrow-based. It was connected to the umbilical area by a band, so they cut the band. After all of that, her tummy area should be fine. At 5:45 p.m. I met the main pediatric surgeon, Dr. Andrassy, who seemed like he really cared about Karen and all her problems. His assistants came in to quickly check Karen at 6:00.

Later, Dr. Young came in and said that Karen would be able to move out of PCCU and to a room on Saturday. She also said that if looks could kill, she would be dead on the floor with the one Karen gave her that morning. She then explained that Thursday night she kept telling Karen to breathe on her own when they needed to put the second ventilator tube down her, hoping to prevent the need for it. She said that Karen gave her a look like, "I feel just fine on all this medication. Forget it!" Just a little stubborn, isn't she! (I wonder where she gets that?)

My husband brought the girls to visit at 8:30 p.m. A nurse had told them that Karen would be in a room, and they would be able to see her there. (Children were not able to visit siblings in PCCU until they had counseled with a child psychologist who would determine their readiness to visit PCCU.) When I started rocking Karen at 4:30 after her ventilator tube was out, I had forgotten to call Pat before his office closed at 5:00 to tell him that the doctors decided to leave Karen in PCCU longer because of the delay in getting her tube out. When they arrived, the girls were upset, because they could not see Karen. My husband was even more upset, because I had not called him to tell him of the changes.

Because he was tired and frustrated, he could not decide whether to go home or to stay in Houston at a motel, so that he and the girls could see Karen the next day. When they told me that Karen might be transferred to the general pediatrics unit right after lunch the next day, he must have been considering taking me home with them, because he then said that he could not get me back in time if he had to drink too much coffee to drive home. He even suggested that I drive them home. Bewildered, I told him that I was too tired to drive, so I would just stay at the hospital to be there when they transferred Karen to a room, and that he could do whatever he wanted. He decided to go home. I was hurt and felt like I was being blamed for the whole misunderstanding about where Karen would be and for his being too tired to go home or to come back the next day. Why did they get there so late anyway? At least that wasn't my fault! None of it seemed to make sense!

On Saturday, I woke up at 8:30 a.m. and was ready by 9:20.

Unfortunately, they didn't let me in to see Karen, because they had already started rounds. Since I hadn't realized that doctor's rounds didn't start at 10:00 a.m. on the weekend, as well as during the week, I couldn't see her until noon. I was discouraged again.

At 1:00 p.m. Karen was moved to room 3421, right next door to her last room, and in the room in which Josh had been. (He was nine years old and had a malignant brain tumor, of which most, but not all, was removed. Parents in the PCCU lobby shared many of the facts and frustrations about their children with other parents.) I had a chance to rock Karen a little bit, but she acted like she felt terrible. Although the nurses gave her some Tylenol for pain at 3:00 and again sometime between 8:00 and 9:00 p.m., she was still fussy and had a difficult time going to sleep.

In the afternoon, I had talked to a chaplain named John *Jack* Dugan. (I had talked to him Thursday or Friday night about the nurses after Karen's surgery, when I had not been notified that they had finished her surgery and had taken her to PCCU.) I told Jack about how upset my husband had been with me for not calling him at work, for wanting to stay at the hospital Friday night, for wanting him to help me by staying at the hospital for me on Saturday, and for his unspoken need for me to try to find time to be with him. Although my husband had not been saying much lately, his frustrations were obvious; I felt like he was taking his frustrations out on me. I was exhausted and having a difficult time, too. Since Jack had decided to become a priest after his wife had died, he understood a lot about marital problems. He told me that I would have to remember just one thing, that men can sometimes be such ———. (I truly do not remember the precise word he used, but it was appropriate and perfect at the time. It probably was not the kind of word that most priests would have used either, unless they were as down-to-earth and understanding as Jack.) I certainly appreciated talking to Jack; he was a great sounding board for me.

When I hurt, he could make me laugh or put things in a more proper perspective. Being a hospital chaplain was some of the last training he needed for him to become a priest. He was going to be a great priest!

Mom, Dad, and Grandma Lucy came to the hospital before 6:00 p.m. Later, we all went to the cafeteria for dinner, and by 7:10 I went to look for my husband and daughters. They were just arriving, and he surprised me by being prepared to spend the night with Karen as I had requested the night before. The visit with everyone really cheered me up, and Mom had the opportunity to meet Dr. Aceves. When we returned to the room, Karen seemed to be doing fine.

The girls and I left at 9:15 p.m. and got home by 10:30. I did one load of laundry and went to bed at 11:30. Since Kimi had fallen asleep in the car, I had already put her into her bed. Stephanie slept with me. Kimi came into my room around 3:00 a.m. and said that she was having a bad dream—about sleeping beauty and the bad witch. We all snuggled up in my bed.

On Sunday, I had awakened at 7:20 a.m., but did not even try to get ready for church, because all of my clothes for the hospital needed to be cleaned. I finally got out of bed at 8:30, started a load of laundry, and went back to bed until 9:40. When I got up then, I woke up the girls. Eventually I washed two loads of clothes and one of sheets, unloaded and loaded the dishwasher, folded and hung up clothes, and fed the dogs. All of us cleaned up, washed and dried our hair, and had brunch at 11:30 a.m. We finally arrived at the hospital at 4:20 p.m.

Pat said that Karen had slept okay from 4:00 to 8:30 a.m. and later for a couple more hours. She sounded so congested that I wondered how she had slept well at all.

My nephew, Shane, and Mom, Dad, and Grandma all came to visit late Sunday afternoon. Mom told me that Stacey and Steve, my brother, had come to Grandma's earlier. They had become proud parents of a baby boy, Christopher Sean, on April 8. Mom also said that my sister, Carol, would hopefully be getting a new and better job soon. Unfortunately, Carol's mother-in-law, Esther Moreno, had been diagnosed with terminal cancer and was given only a few months to a year to live. Roy and Carol knew this, but Esther didn't know yet! It felt good to *catch up* on family news. Before everyone else left, Pat had to leave with the girls, because he needed to arrange for a babysitter for the girls for the next day.

By evening, Karen's oxygen level was low, mostly in the 70s and 80s, and she was still extremely congested. Doctors put her back under an oxygen hood, began checking her carbon dioxide (CO_2) level (which stimulates respiration at normal rates of fifty to seventy breaths per minute)[3] and her oxygen saturation (SATs) more often, and increased her respiratory treatments and the amount of Lasix they were giving her. (Lasix is a diuretic drug to reduce the fluid volume in the blood and body tissues and is anti-hypertensive to lower blood pressure. It was probably used to reduce the fluid content in her lungs.)[4]

Karen didn't sleep well Monday morning between midnight and 5:00 a.m. The nurses woke me up at 6:00 a.m. to tell me that her IV was not working, and they would have to put in another one. They finished quickly, and Karen went back to sleep. Their skill and her comfort were both an answer to prayer.

Karen began running a fever of 101°. She continued to have a lot of congestion in her nose and chest, and her SATs were low, in the 80s. Dr. Thapar, her cardiologist, said that he would need to examine the x-rays that they had done in the morning before he would know what was wrong. Her fever continued all day between 101° and 103.2°F. They scheduled blood tests to determine if bacteria were present in her lungs and which type. It might be another form of pneumonia; it might not be. Dr. Aceves said that it could have been a germ she picked up at the hospital after or during surgery, because that happens at hospitals sometimes. They would probably start her on general antibiotics and in a few days after the blood cultures were done, then they could give her a more specific antibiotic.

They discussed starting her on Pedialyte, because she was probably hungry, and it might make her feel and sleep better. (I think that they had discontinued her formula when she started running a higher fever.) If they started feeding her through the tube, they could use the IV for medicine. If they kept the IV for nutrients, they might need to insert a special IV for medication.

A doctor had come in earlier that day and asked me questions about Karen. I had asked him if he were Dr. Andrassy and explained that I did not recognize him for sure, since the last time I had seen him he had had on scrubs and a surgery covering tied on his head. (Then he was wearing slacks, a sport shirt, and suspenders.) He laughed and said that was better than what one lady had told him. She said that she did not recognize him with clothes on—and her big husband was in the room at the time and gave them both a funny look.

On Tuesday, June 13, Karen's fever started going up to 103° and then to 105°. They tried to do a lot of blood work, but had a difficult time getting blood, since Karen's veins were so little. The doctor in charge called in different interns, residents, and nurses to *give it a try.* Karen's SATs were going down, too. She started breathing hard and her pulse got very fast. The doctor kept insisting that they needed to get blood for tests, even when her tiny body was under a lot of stress and she was screaming. (At one time her SATs were down to only 61%, and her pulse was up to 179, compared to a normal pulse for babies of 115 to 140, according to her doctors.) I suggested that they let her calm down a little before trying anymore. Since the blood would be used mainly to check her SATs and CO_2 levels, which obviously were not good according to the monitors, what was the point of the test, except to put numbers on a piece of paper? Reluctantly, they waited a very short time before trying again. Finally, someone from PCCU got some blood from Karen early in the morning. (Their records coldly stated, "On June 13 she began to experience a fever, became tachypneic and had retractions. She was started on antibiotic therapy for possible staph and pseudomonas consisting of… " various medications. Tachypnea is abnormal rapidity of breathing which, if prolonged, could cause excess loss of CO_2 and lead to hyperventilation. A retraction is a *sucking in* of the skin around the neck, collarbone, or rib cage.)[5]

By then, the nurse in charge of that section of the pediatrics floor recommended that the doctor in charge for the evening put Karen back in PCCU, because she needed more care than they were able to give her. The doctor, a resident, did not want her moving back and forth between the floor and PCCU and felt that he could handle the crisis, that it was only temporary. I told him that I trusted my children's lives to their pediatrician, but that he knew his limits and the limits of the hospital in Lake Jackson. That was why Karen was at Hermann then. I don't think that he appreciated the parallel that I was attempting to draw for him.

Karen was fidgety and had not slept since early that morning. She finally calmed down a little near 3:30 a.m. after a breathing treatment, and I lay down to rest. I was startled out of my sleep between 7:30 and 8:00 a.m., when I heard Verna, one of the nurses, say that they needed to change her IV, because it was out again.

Exasperated, I called Sally Olsen to come and look at Karen. She and Dr. Aceves got there as quickly as possible. (They had been making rounds, and she dropped her books and spilled her coffee when she heard what had happened that night and early morning.) They decided to move Karen back into PCCU. At first they put her under an oxygen hood, but then decided to put a ventilator tube back down her throat to help her breathe. Parts of her lungs were having trouble getting air and were collapsed. (Medical terms on her records were impersonal, "required reintubation following respiratory distress.") They also put a direct line into her artery (an ART line) in her right wrist by making an incision and sewing the tubing in. They would then use that to take blood for tests, rather than poking her for blood each time.

On Wednesday I was exhausted. Because I didn't wake up until 11:00 a.m., I couldn't go into PCCU to see Karen until 12:30 or 1:00 p.m., after the doctors' rounds. There, Dr. Aceves told me that a large area of her right lung was congested and deflated. The doctors determined that she had aspiration pneumonia again, probably from getting food in her lungs before or during surgery.

In the evening, her forehead started getting puffier and had reddish purple areas on it, because the IV on the top of her head began infiltrating. (The solution in the IV had begun going into the subcutaneous tissue rather than into the vein.)[6] If the problem was not corrected when the IV was repositioned, they said that they might need to sew a central line into her vein, too. This was all getting to be too much for me. I didn't go to bed until 11:30 p.m.

On Thursday, June 15, I woke up at 8:20 a.m. After I cleaned up, I went to see Karen at 9:00 a.m. Dr. Young told me that Karen's lungs were sounding good and her right lung had reinflated. Unfortunately, because the IV on the left side of her head had infiltrated more during the night or early morning, the left side of her head was quite swollen. They had taken out both IV's in her head and put one in her neck on the right side. They picked that side, because she liked to sleep with her head to the left. Karen slept the whole time I was there until rounds started at 10:00 a.m.

In the lobby, Chaplain Jack told me that I ought to go home to get some rest and spend time with my other girls, so that when Karen went back out to the floor, I would be rested enough to help her. When I told Pat the idea, he planned to get the work phone number of one of the men from church who worked in Houston, so that I could get a ride back to Lake Jackson with him. Then my husband would bring the girls and me back the next day. It seemed like a good plan, but he wasn't able to get the phone number that day.

Karen's nose and mouth had a lot of secretions to be suctioned (especially in her mouth because of the ventilator tube). Her head started looking a little better in the evening as the swelling went down. They reduced her oxygen from 75% to 40% and her respirations from fifteen to thirteen per minute. The machines needed to do less. They hoped to get her off the ventilator the next day.

They finally started her on Pedialyte, first in a feeding tube in her nose and then through her G-tube (the gastrostomy tube). If she did fine, they would alternate Pedialyte with formula. She would have food again.

I made a Scripture flip chart on healing, faith, and encouragement, for moms and other family members of children (or even adults) in hospitals, especially in critical care units. I got the idea from talking to other parents and grandparents, mostly to moms. Because many of our friends had written down Scriptures for us or told us different Scriptures to read for ourselves and for Karen when we first discovered that she had Trisomy 18, I had decided to write them all on spiraled index cards, rather than having to look them up each time. I wrote them in large letters to make them easier for me to read any time of the day or night, in any degree of alertness, in dimly lit rooms, and with a wiggling crying baby. The spirals made them easy to put down quickly and to still keep my place. I took the verses from several of my booklets and compiled one that would not be specific to our problems or Karen's, but could apply to anyone. I worked on the booklet most of the night, arranging various Scriptures until the sequence seemed to flow from one to the next, and then writing them on

4 x 6 spiraled index cards. I finally finished the booklet at about midnight, Thursday, June 15.

On Friday, Karen was still on the ventilator. They had put her back up to 75% oxygen and fifteen respirations per minute during the night, but had reduced the oxygen back down to 50% by the time I saw her. Doctors hoped to get her off the ventilator by the weekend.

CHAPTER SEVEN

Going Home to Rest?

S ally Olsen and Chaplain Jack continued to tell me that I needed to go home for the weekend. My husband had planned to bring Kimi and Stephanie Friday night at 7:00 to talk to Richard Weir, the Child Life psychologist, about PCCU, in order for them to be able to visit Karen in PCCU, since it began to seem like she would be in there a lot. However, he called in the morning and said that he had an appointment at 4:30 p.m., which would make it difficult for him to get to Houston by 7:00. I should try to get a ride with Hugh Mauldin, the man from church who worked in Houston. Unfortunately, Hugh's secretary said that he was in Pearland and might not come back to the office. I called John, our pastor, at 11:30 a.m., and he told me that he would have someone at the hospital at 1:30 p.m. When I stayed with Karen from 12:30 to 1:15 p.m., she was a little congested, but okay. The nurses told me that she would be fine and to have a good time at home. When I got outside, our pastor picked me up himself.

I had called Pat to let him know my plans for coming home. He and Bami tidied the house. At 3:00 p.m. I got home and called Bami, and she brought the girls home around 4:15. When my husband got home between 5:30 and 6:00, the girls and I were in the den reading and thought that he would come back to join us. However, he had expected us to come into the living room and was upset because we had not greeted him at the door. Rather than being glad like the girls were that I was home, he went straight into the extra bedroom to take a nap. He got up from his nap as I was getting the girls and myself ready for bed and told Kimi that she could sleep with me, because he would sleep in the extra bedroom. We both expected a "welcome home" and got a real shock! By trying to make our desires someone else's goals, whether they knew or understood them or not, we had unmet expectations and frustrations on both sides.

Saturday morning Pat called the hospital, and the nurses told him that Karen was fine. We could enjoy the weekend without worrying about her.

On Saturday, I tried to sleep late, but had a difficult time. Stephanie was getting ready from 8:00 to 9:30 a.m. to clog at Creekfest. Her friend Shelly's mom took her, and brought her home at noon. One of the things about Karen's extended illness that really broke my heart was not being able to watch Stephanie dance with the other Bluebonnet Cloggers whenever they went places to perform. She was a talented little dancer with a natural rhythm and grace, and a smile that said that she loved dancing. When Karen was home, I could seldom take her places, because her immune system was immature and made it unsafe for her to be around a lot of people, especially children, who carried all the normal childhood germs. When Karen was in the hospital, I was normally there with her. Consequently, unless my husband or a friend could watch Karen, I missed most of Stephanie's clogging performances. This time I was just too exhausted.

I washed clothes and played with Kimi in the morning. After Stephanie got home we all had lunch. Stephanie went to a friend's from 1:30 to 4:00 p.m., and I got my hair cut at 1:30. Kimi want-ed to play with Alison, one of the neighbors, but her mother said that she would not be back until 2:00. At 3:00 when she got home, she had to take a nap. Kimi was understandably upset, because she had waited so long for nothing. The girls and I went shopping at the mall from 5:30 to 9:00 and bought dinner to take home, but my husband had not wanted to go. He was upset with me for spending so much time with the girls and not resting. However, he had not made any effort to do anything with me or with us all, and didn't understand that it was relaxing to me just to be able to go to the mall and look at things and laugh and have fun. When we got home, Pat and I talked a little while, and I cried a lot. I needed sup-porting and sharing, not this.

On Sunday morning, I woke up at 6:00 a.m. and worked on the laundry until about 7:00. I couldn't sleep; I just cried and went back to bed. When we woke up for church, my husband and I were final-ly on amicable terms again, although it was more accommodating than friendly. We all went to church. At greeting time Kathy Foh, who was sitting in front of us, asked me if Karen was still in the hos-pital. When Charlotte Stark sang *Amazing Grace*, I started weeping, left my seat, and went to the ladies' room. Janis Warny was sitting behind us and came in to talk with me awhile. I finally calmed down and went back into the sanctuary for the sermon. After the service, our family went to eat Chinese food for lunch and really enjoyed it. When we got home, I was exhausted and took a nap. At 2:45 I got up and packed, and we left by 3:30. We ran errands, took Stephanie to her dad's, and arrived at the hospital by 6:00, where my husband and I took turns seeing Karen and watching Kimi in the lobby.

Karen looked all right, but was sleeping. She had gotten off the ventilator at noon and was under an oxygen hood. She even had the staples taken out of her gastrostomy incision. She had been a busy baby while we were gone! Since she was asleep, we decided to leave the hospital to eat dinner, run more errands, and get Stephanie from her dad's. When my family dropped me off at the hospital at 9:30 p.m., the security lady at the door on the first floor had to make two calls to the nurses' stations to make sure that it was okay for me to come upstairs. Then the elevator took another five minutes to get me to the pediatrics floor. By the time I waited for all of that, I forgot that I was supposed to have called Bami after 10:30 to let her know that my family was on the way to her house. By the time I remembered, they were probably there anyway. Did I really relax and rest?

CHAPTER EIGHT

Why Am I Still Here?

But sanctify Christ as Lord in your hearts, always being ready to make a defense to everyone who asks you to give an account for the hope that is in you, yet with gentleness and reverence (1 Pet. 3:15 NASB).

I was beginning to wonder why we were still at the hospital. Karen got over pneumonia and got her gastrostomy, and then got sick again. She would seem to be well, only to have trouble again and end up back in PCCU. Although I still believed that God was in charge and was taking care of her, I didn't understand all the changes. Why couldn't she get well and stay well?

Sunday night, Karen seemed to be breathing a little harder. Her nurse, Marsha, said that her SATs were lower and her temperature was slightly low, but had been up and down most of the day. At 11:30 her breathing became more difficult; she got restless and started crying. They gave her a breathing treatment, which caused her to cough a lot, a sign that the junk in her lungs was loosening up and trying to come out. Then they took an x-ray, which looked better than earlier, but still showed that she had pneumonia. At 1:00 a.m. they gave her another breathing treatment and scheduled them for every two hours after that. She finally started breathing better by 1:45 a.m. By then, she was also more awake and restless, but the medicine had a tendency to cause that. She was still crying too, but not as much as before. I finally gave up and went to the sleep room at 1:50 a.m., but then had to wait for another mom, who was up late taking her turn in the parents' bathroom. Exhausted, but restless, I went to bed at 2:30 a.m.

On Monday, June 19, I saw Karen in the morning—hyper again, and crying. They had increased her oxygen to almost 75%. Her breathing was better, but still not good. She sounded congested, but not as much as earlier. Her SATs were in the mid to high 80s; her pulse was high, in the 170s. I didn't want to leave her when they started rounds at 10:15, because she was fussy, but I knew that there was nothing I could do. I had to leave her, knowing only that she was in God's hands.

As I left PCCU, I saw an 18-year-old single mom, Rhonda, and talked with her awhile about her baby, Desierae, who had Down's syndrome and heart problems. Rhonda wanted to go to church with her baby and do the right thing for her, but she said that she didn't even know what church she should go to. I explained that what church denomination she attended was not as important as simply being a Christian and having a personal relationship with the Lord. She didn't have to be the same denomination that her parents were, especially since they didn't go enough for her to even know what denomination they belonged to. I also told her that it was important for her to go to church, pray, and read her Bible regularly. Then I gave her the Scripture spiral booklet that I had written a few days earlier. I was ready to talk to her about salvation when one of her friends came in.

Karen was still having problems breathing. They increased her respiratory treatments and increased her oxygen to 80%, but the medications were making her hyper. Theresa, one of the nurses, gave her medicine to calm her down a little. I talked to Sally and Dr. Aceves about possible heart surgery for Karen. Many risks were involved whether we had surgery or not. She and several of the doctors wanted to discuss the possibilities and risks with my husband and me the next day at 2:00 p.m.

My best friend since fourth grade, Maura, brought lasagna for dinner, and we went to the cafeteria to eat. I appreciated having Maura come to visit me. Although we often wouldn't see each other for a year or more, if we needed each other, we were always there. When we got back to the room, Karen's breathing was still difficult and her heart rate was high. She looked like she might not make it through the night; she was so pale and extremely agitated. The IV in her foot had already come out, and they were unable to get another one in. I suggested that they ask a Turner nurse to try, since the Turner unit cares for neonatal babies with problems. Karen's nurse, Debbie, said that the doctors told her that if she couldn't get the IV in with one try, they would put a direct line into her vein. Debbie and another nurse, Marsha, had poked several times in the same hole trying to find Karen's tiny vein. Maura and I left Karen's room at 10:30, and Maura went home. After I read awhile, I went to bed at 11:15.

On Tuesday, June 20, I woke up at 6:15 a.m. and went to see Karen between 6:20 and 6:45. They did an x-ray on her chest and had tried to put a line into a vein in her wrist, but couldn't. Finally they put a direct line into the vein in her right thigh by making an incision and sewing it in like they did the ART line. Seeing her two incisions made me hurt! They had put her on the ventilator again, with twenty-five respirations per minute and 83% oxygen. She was also taking formula in her G-tube. Her breathing appeared better, and she was more relaxed. When I had gone to bed the night before, I had admitted that I couldn't do any more for her by sitting and watching her. I left her room, prayed for her in my room, went back to sleep at 7:00 a.m., and stayed in bed until noon. I woke up a few times, but was so exhausted that I kept going back to sleep. I finally got up, cleaned up, and went to see Karen at 1:30 p.m. Sally Olsen and my husband got there at 2:00.

The doctors conferred first, and then met with us. Dr. Young (from PCCU), Dr. Thapar (the cardiologist), Dr. Greenhaw (a female geneticist), and Sally Olsen spoke with us. Karen's chances without heart surgery were about zero. The mortality rate of surgery was about 20 to 25%. Surgery might not be successful and completely cure the problem or might not cure the problem at all. Because of Karen's Trisomy 18, they would have to talk to the surgeons at Texas Children's Hospital and see if they were even willing to do surgery. She might be severely mentally retarded and a burden on us later, because she would not be able to take care of herself. It might not look like she was mentally retarded then, but it could show up later. Her development might even stop. Were we willing to take that responsibility? My husband and I felt that she deserved a chance to live as normal a life as possible, and that she should have that chance. They would check with the surgeons and arrange for surgery, when and if she were more stable. I went back to talk to Rhonda about salvation. I went through the salvation plan that was in our church brochure, but Sally Olsen and another nurse got there before we could pray. Sally said that my pastor had gone to buy coffee and was looking for me.

John had been in Karen's room, praying for her and waiting for us. He and I left Karen's room and found Pat in the cafeteria, and we all talked awhile. John bought lunch for Sharon, Karen's nurse, because she had been such a helpful, caring nurse. Later, Pat and I went back to the room to see Karen and then went to eat.

When we returned, we saw my brother, Phil, and his son, Kevin, in the lobby. Dad was going in for surgery the next day at 10:00 a.m., because he had a malignant tumor on his colon. Doctors discovered it the previous Friday, when he had gone to the hospital for tests after he had been bleeding when he went to the bathroom. I called Dad at the hospital, and he was in good spirits. I told him that we would pray for him, and he said that he would pray for Karen. He explained that Friday had been *show and tell* from about 4:00 p.m. to 6:00 p.m. for him and for Mom. Pat and I prayed for Karen a little while, and then after he left, I read Scriptures to her quietly. Her oxygen was increased to 100%, and her respirations were still twenty-five per minute. They had switched her from morphine to a medication that would help her agitation more than her pain, because she still had not been sleeping well with the morphine. I left her room just before 10:00 p.m. and called our pastor's daughter, Kim Haynes, to put Dad's surgery and Rhonda's salvation on the prayer chain. How much more could I take—first Karen, now Dad?

Rhonda was not in her room, but was getting ready to leave the next day. Before she left, I wanted to exchange addresses and give her the Gospel of John booklet that Pastor John had brought me. I had given her the Scripture booklet I made earlier, because she liked it so much, and a Hagin booklet, *Don't Blame God*. Before lunch, I found her, exchanged addresses and phone numbers, and gave her the new booklet. Her friend with her then said that his dad was a fundamentalist Baptist preacher and that he wanted some day to be a missionary, possibly in Zaire or somewhere else in Africa. I hoped that he would also be able to talk more to her about God.

On Wednesday, Karen was still on the ventilator. Her respirations per minute were set between fifteen and twenty and her oxygen varied between 75% and 80% most of the day. Her SATs were only in the 80s, and her heart rate was normal, in the 140s to 150s. She was finally sleeping a lot. Dr. Young said that Karen had been getting formula in her G-tube, but they had discontinued it when they put the ventilator in the day before. However, they would be starting her back on formula again that day, with potassium chloride and sodium chloride added to her formula, although I wasn't sure why.

Dad was at Round Rock Hospital, where my sister Carol's husband, Roy, worked. His surgery had been scheduled for Wednesday morning, and he had already returned to his room by 2:10 p.m. when I called. He was not quite awake, but sounded like he hurt. When I talked to Phil, he said that Dad's surgery had gone well. They had removed a section of his colon, and there were no visible signs that the cancer had spread outside of the colon. They were waiting for pathology reports to come back the next day.

I got a ride home with Hugh Mauldin near 6:00 p.m. Pat and I ate and visited from 7:00 to 8:30 and then picked up the girls from Bami's. I had decided to try a different plan that time. I would visit with my husband before the girls came home, to make him feel more important.

On Thursday, June 22, Stephanie and Kimi and I met Maura and her son, Clayton, at 1:00 p.m. at Hermann Hospital to celebrate Karen's six-month birthday. (Because many Trisomy-18 babies didn't even reach their first month, we felt that getting halfway to a year was a major accomplishment!) We all visited with Richard Weir, the child psychologist. He and I looked at Karen first and determined what types of wires, tubes, and machines were attached to her. He had a baby doll that he showed our children, and they got to help him connect the same or similar attachments to the doll that were connected to Karen. That would help them understand what to expect when they saw her. After we met with Richard, we rushed to the cafeteria, but it had already closed after lunch. We bought some chips from the snack machines before we went upstairs to see Karen. Stephanie held Karen's hand and was very conscious of all the wires and attachments and did not want anyone (especially Kimi) to get too close to them. She was trying to be very grown up about the whole situation. Kimi almost ignored the wires and just patted Karen's head and held her hand. She saw simply that Karen was her baby sister. Then she got her face right down close to Karen's and talked and sang to her. Richard got tickled at the way both girls interacted with Karen and said that it was just like I had anticipated: Stephanie had been very attentive and helpful while putting things on the baby doll and Kimi had acted like she could care less. She had hardly paid any attention to the doll. Their personalities as well as their ages made a big difference in the way they acted. (Kimi was four; Stephanie was ten.) We all finally went to eat lunch after 3:00 p.m. and then went back to the PCCU lobby for Karen's *half-birthday* cake. Maura and Clayton left after the cake, and the girls and I went back in the room to visit with Karen. We left after 6:00 p.m.

On Friday, Dr. Thapar was scheduled to meet with four members of Texas Children's Hospital staff at 9:00 a.m. He had told Sally that he would call me back near noon. Since I was not going to be at the hospital, she suggested that I start calling him near 11:00 a.m. After I called, he had gone to the hospital to talk with me, not realizing that I was at home. We eventually talked on the phone. He said that their answer was "No," and that I should call them for details and ask for the cardiologist in charge. When I called their office, the secretary said that there were about twenty cardiologists and that the man in charge was on vacation, but his next in line was Dr. Smith (not his real name). We could talk to him on the phone or come in to speak with him in person, for which there would be a charge. She sounded so negative that it seemed to be a deterrent, like she felt we would be wasting his time. I talked with Dr. Smith, and he said that they had decided not to operate on Karen because her Trisomy 18 was lethal anyway. Their basic feeling was, "Why bother?" When I asked if the decision was based on the condition of her heart, or simply the Trisomy 18, he said that the decision was based on her trisomy disorder. However, my husband and I could talk with him in person if we wished, or both of us could talk to him on the phone. They preferred not to talk to only one parent at a time. Needless to say, I was extremely upset when I called my husband. He left work early so that we could go talk to Dr. Smith in person. We took Kimi to Jana's, and dropped off Stephanie at her dad's in Houston. By the time we arrived at Hermann Hospital at 4:00 p.m. and saw Karen, we changed our minds about seeing Dr. Smith. It would be a waste of money to see a doctor who seemed so opposed to our daughter's surgery. Was she a baby or a statistic?

We found Dr. Carvajal, head of PCCU, and Dr. Aceves and spoke with them. They seemed to think that we should talk with Dr. Smith to at least get the details or total reasoning behind the decision. Dr. Carvajal even suggested that we speak with the ethics committee for the hospitals and get their opinion. Sometimes doctors were encouraged or forced to do procedures by the committee because of ethical reasons. Dr. Aceves also suggested that we think about how far and how hard we wanted to push for the surgery. What if complications would leave Karen on the ventilator for the rest of her life or would disable her further? Would we be willing to stop at some point? What did we want for ourselves and for Karen? Basically, I told him that we would have to take each step as we came to it, one day at a time. We wouldn't want to leave her permanently or drastically disabled just to keep her *alive*. That wouldn't be right for her either. At that point we needed more facts or opinions about her heart before we could make an intelligent decision. I couldn't understand why a doctor wouldn't want to do surgery simply because a baby had Trisomy 18, if the condition of her heart warranted surgery. Unfortunately, my husband had called the doctor's secretary earlier to cancel our appointment with him, because we had thought that the conversation would be futile.

After Dr. Carvajal and Dr. Aceves changed our minds, we were unable to reach Dr. Smith's office. We left the hospital at 9:20 p.m., after we had gone back to see Karen for about 45 more minutes.

On Saturday, my husband and I arrived at Texas Children's Hospital (TCH) between 10:00 and 10:30 a.m., hoping to talk to Dr. Smith without an appointment. The man at the information desk in the lobby said that we couldn't see him, because no one was in the office and he wasn't the doctor on call. Frustrated again, we left TCH and went to Hermann to see Karen.

We called Texas Children's later to talk to the cardiologist on call to determine if he knew about Karen, since we had been told that Dr. Smith was not there. Dr. Brown (not his real name) said that he knew about Karen and would check with the staff there and call back. A female doctor, Dr. Jones (not her real name), called us back and gave us a lot of details about Karen's heart and lungs and said that she had recommended not doing surgery for the following reasons:

- The echocardiogram and electrocardiogram (EKG) that Dr. Jones saw did not make Karen a good candidate for surgery. (An EKG is a record of the electrical activity of the heart and is valuable in diagnosing abnormal cardiac rhythm and damage to the heart muscle.)

- Karen's VSD was large and extensive, and both sides of her heart wall were thickened because of the extra workload. Because of the large hole, the pressure on one side of her heart was one fifth of that on the other side. The pressure on one side should be slightly higher, because there would not be much flow if the pressures were equal, but her difference was significant. This caused the pressures in her lungs to be so high also that she could easily die of pulmonary hypertension. If persistent, she could stay on a ventilator or possibly maximum support for the rest of her life, which might not be long without surgery.

- The surgery would be extremely risky even for a normal child with Karen's heart, but Karen's Trisomy 18 just made it worse, like asking the surgeon to be the executioner. A complete patch or repair of her heart didn't look like a real option, and banding was eventually ruled out also. (The surgeon puts a *band* on the pulmonary artery to slow down the blood flow to the lungs, so they wouldn't easily become congested.)[7] Many Trisomy-18 children die of cardiac problems; most that don't die have minor or no heart defects. Dr. Jones felt that Karen wouldn't survive surgery. Without it, she might at least live a little while. (But with what quality of life?)

Four staff members of TCH talked with Dr. Thapar and based their decision on Karen's genetic defect. Now we had several opinions on which to base our decision: that of Dr. Smith and his staff, that of Dr. Brown (part of that staff), and that of Dr. Thapar, who suggested a 50% risk or higher. It was time to get another more positive opinion, if possible, especially since her chances without surgery seemed to be *zero*.

Maura suggested we contact a friend of her sister's who was head of the Texas Branch of Rights for Mentally Retarded and Handicapped Children. Others suggested we call Marvin Zindler. Sally Olsen and Dr. Aceves seemed to think that doing any of that would be a waste of our energy then, but perhaps something to consider later. It made more sense at that time to avoid negative contacts and stay in touch with positive people, like Dr. Simpson, to whom Sally referred us, (and them). Pat and I left the hospital at 6:30 p.m., bought some chicken at the mall, picked up Kimi at Jana's, and went home, totally drained.

On Sunday, June 25, we went to church and told our pastor what the various doctors had said and explained that we either needed for surgery to be possible and for a doctor able and willing to do it, or we needed a total miracle on Karen's heart and lungs. I went to the front of the church during prayer time for prayer for healing of my sinuses and aching back, and Kimi went with me, because she said that she had something stuck in her throat that she couldn't get out herself. (I think that she just wanted to be with me.) Craig prayed for me and then prayed for our family to rest in God's love, trust Him, and know that He loved us. John called my husband and me forward for prayer in proxy for Karen and asked all to agree with us for a doctor willing and able to do surgery on Karen to correct her heart.

That afternoon, Pat, Kimi, and I went to the hospital to visit Karen, who was doing better. Kimi talked and sang to Karen and played with her toys. Since Stephanie's dad was at work and his girlfriend, Doris, didn't have a car, she was unable to bring Stephanie to the hospital to visit, too. We stayed in Karen's room from 4:00 to 6:20, and then called Margaret Kana to baby-sit with Kimi for the next week.

Grandma Lucy came to the hospital to take me to a choir performance at her church. Their choir would be leaving on Tuesday to tour Hungary, Austria, and Switzerland. Kimi and my husband had the opportunity to tell Grandma "Hi" when she arrived, and Kimi said that she wanted to go, too. However, Grandma told her she was delighted to see her, but she felt that Kimi would not be able to sit still and be quiet enough for the entire performance. Kimi reluctantly agreed. When they left, they stopped to get Stephanie from her dad's. The choir's singing was beautiful!

When I returned from the concert, I stayed in Karen's room from 10:00 p.m. until midnight, because she was alert and finally calmed down. I shared a parent sleep room with a lady named Trucine, whose 10-year-old son was also in PCCU for his heart.

On Monday, Karen's oxygen level from the ventilator had remained stable near 40% for over twenty-four hours. Her respirations by machine were still thirty and would be gradually reduced to ten, until she would be doing most of the breathing on her own. They would extubate her (take the ventilator tube out) as soon as possible, maybe that night or the next day. I talked to the nutritionist about using Polycose to supplement Karen's formula to help her gain weight more rapidly. Dr. Allen had used it when she was at home. Since the nutritionist said that Dr. Carvajal didn't approve over 17 calories per ounce for infants, I talked with him. He said that they would extubate her first, and then consider increasing her calories.

Dr. Smith called me in the afternoon and said that he had tried four numbers before he located me. He had been at the hospital Friday, but did not get our note about canceling the meeting with him until after 7:00 p.m. (as if his office's inefficiency was our fault!). I told him that we had decided not to see him when we first arrived, because of his negative attitude, but some of the doctors at Hermann had convinced us to speak with him simply to get more information. Unfortunately, the people we spoke with Friday evening and Saturday morning said that we couldn't see him, because he wasn't in the office or on call. We had no way of knowing that they were wrong. Later, we had decided to see if the person on call could give us any information about Karen. Dr. Smith then insisted that we shouldn't be trying to talk to all nineteen of the other doctors, but should talk with him only. (We weren't trying for all nineteen, just one!) He then stated that I had wasted Dr. Brown's time, which he should have been spending with his patients. After his lengthy explanation and reprimand, he again remarked that he wouldn't speak to only one parent on the phone and asked if we still wanted to talk with him in person? When I told him that my husband was busy too and would have to call him to arrange a time convenient for both of them, he said that he would just wait until he got a call from my husband. That man was so rude! When I later told Dr. Aceves about the conversation, he said it would probably be best not to talk with that doctor anymore, because he would be biased and negative, and it would be simply a waste of our time.

I talked with Esther in Dr. Simpson's office in Corpus Christi about surgery on Karen's heart. She was waiting to talk with Dr. Thapar again and then would call me back. Before I left Karen's room at 6:30, they had reduced her respirations to fifteen. Since Dr. Sharon had called for me from Corpus when I left to eat dinner, I called her back. She said that she and Dr. Simpson felt that Karen would be a good candidate for pulmonary arterial banding, one of the techniques that Dr. Jones at TCH had mentioned earlier. She said that if Karen got weaned off the ventilator and was stable, and if Dr. Carvajal approved it and we agreed to the transfer, Karen could go to the hospital in Corpus Christi. They would be able to do surgery early that week or after the 4th of July. Here was an answer to prayer! Sally knew Dr. Simpson and had told us that not only was he a fine surgeon, but he was a great person as well. I was so excited that I called Pat, Grandma, and Phil. Mom called me before I had a chance to call her. (Dad was recovering well and would be going home on Wednesday.) Pat would check with the insurance company and CIDC (Chronically Ill and Disabled Children) to see if the transfer would be approved and covered.

Karen was taken off the ventilator at 7:50 p.m., while I was at dinner. She was under the hood at 60% oxygen initially and then 45% later. When I walked in, she was lying on her tummy. I almost cried. She looked more comfortable than she had looked in a long time. By 9:30 she woke up and fussed until almost 11:30, when they decided to give her a sedative to calm her down. Her SAT's were in the 80s and her heart rate fluctuated from the 150s to the low 190s, a little high. I got to hold her for a while and snuggle her close to me as I stood by the bed and held the oxygen tube to her nose. (She still had a lot of other tubes in and on her.) I left her room before midnight and got to bed after 12:30.

On Tuesday, June 27, Chaplain Jack woke me up at 4:20 a.m. Karen had started having problems at 4:00 a.m.—a Code 3—cardiac arrest! Actually, the nurse had noticed on the monitor that her heart was fibrillating (rapidly quivering in ineffectual contractions)[8]. They did CPR and put her back on the ventilator. She had also looked like she was starting to have a seizure and was acidotic (an acid-base imbalance, abnormally high acidity of the blood; probably related to the ineffective heartbeat and ineffective respirations, causing the oxygen level to drop and the carbon dioxide level to rise)[9]. They had to give her different medications for the various problems. When they were all done, Dr. Guzman explained to me that Karen's heart had not beat for almost two minutes.

Jack and I talked and joked briefly, waiting for the doctors and nurses to clean up Karen. I asked him if he knew the story of Jairus and his daughter in the Bible. Of course, he did. Then I told him that I had dreamed that Karen had died, but was later brought back to life again. Jack started talking about God's will, and I agreed that God's will should be done. We just didn't necessarily agree on what His will was.

I stayed with Karen until after 6:30 a.m. Her hands and feet felt and looked so cold; her arms and hands were purple and mottled. The nurses and I put warm blankets and towels around her and socks on her feet to warm her up. Karen finally relaxed a little, and I went back to bed—and to sleep—at almost 7:00 a.m., after I had called my husband to tell him what had happened.

At 11:00 a.m. I woke up, cleaned up, and went to eat. When I arrived at the room at 12:45, John was there to visit us. He told me that the church would pay the cost of transportation to Corpus Christi if that were our only problem getting her there. He also felt that we should talk more with Dr. Smith or other cardiologists at TCH to convince them to do the surgery. That started getting me frustrated, because it would be a complete change of plans and would be dealing with negative people. I discussed it with Sally, and she agreed with Dr. Aceves that it would be better to go to Corpus and not deal with TCH, because we would probably not change Dr. Smith's mind and it wouldn't be worth the effort trying. My husband spoke to Dr. Thapar, who also didn't feel that we would change anyone's mind. Pat and I agreed that we should stay with the plans for Corpus. That was one of the hardest and most frustrating decisions we ever made.

Finally, I talked to the Life Flight people. Things were set up for the next morning between 8:00 and 8:30 a.m., if a bed were available in ICU in Corpus, and after we would pay an estimated $1,955 for transportation. My husband planned to bring the girls to the hospital that night after he got off work. However, at 7:30 p.m. he called, because he had been spraying the house for fleas and was running late. At 10:00 p.m. they finally arrived to visit with Karen and me. Kimi sang her a song. At 11:00 they left to take Stephanie to her dad's and Kimi to Grandma Lucy's to spend the night. Because they visited with Grandma until after midnight, Pat didn't get back to the hospital until 1:00 a.m., and we finally got to bed at almost 2:00 a.m.

On Wednesday, June 28, Jane, a nurse, woke us up at 6:30 a.m. so that we could get ready to leave by 8:00. At 8:00 they called Corpus: no rooms were available yet, maybe the next day. Later that day the Corpus staff said that maybe they would have a bed near 3:00 p.m. Subsequently they said that they would call if one were available. That night Dr. Carvajal said that it might even be after the 4th before we could go. By then, we just didn't know what might be next; all we could do was wait. My husband picked up Kimi and Stephanie and brought them to the hospital. They were there from 12:15 to 3:30, but Karen was asleep the whole time.

Karen seemed to be breathing well, and they told me that her lungs looked much healthier too. Her SATs were mostly in the 80s, with an oxygen level at 25% and respirations at twenty-five per minute. Later in the afternoon, however, her SATs went down into the 50s. Immediately, Dr. Carvajal put her oxygen up to 100% and said not to set it lower than 40% after that. Karen had slept most of the day. By 10:30, I left the room, read awhile, gave up, and went to bed at 11:00 p.m. I was drained!

On Thursday, I was so tired that I stayed in bed until 10:45 a.m. When I got up, I cleaned up and called Grandma. Then Maura called me as I was debating whether to call her or go to eat. It was encouraging and helpful to talk to family and friends, especially when I had spent the better part of almost a month at the hospital.

Sally came by and said that we might be able to go to Corpus the next day; they might have room then. I went to see Karen at 12:40 p.m., but she was asleep. During the day, her SATs went up and down from the 60s to the 90s, depending on whether or not she was moving, sleeping, or digesting food, and her oxygen varied between 40% and 100%. (Digestion takes a lot of oxygen away from the rest of your body. That's sometimes why we get sleepy after a meal.) In late afternoon Dr. Young said that Karen sounded like she was fighting the ventilator, so they changed her respirations back up to thirty per minute. Because she was sedated a lot, Karen was awake off and on, and looked sad and pleading. She even cried for a little while. She just didn't understand what was happening or why she felt like she did. It hurt to see her like that!

As I talked with the nurses, I found out that the next day would be the last day for Dr. Young and Dr. Guzman in PCCU. Dr. Anna Guzman was going into practice at some clinics in the valley. Dr. Young had finished her studies already, but was a *fellow*, teaching and learning in different units, probably the adult burns unit next. I had a chance to talk to them both before they left, thanking them for all their help and support with Karen.

Maura was supposed to come to the hospital and take me to dinner, but it had been raining so much that I told her not to try. It was such a quiet day. I went to the chapel for a short time in the afternoon—to thank God and ask him to help our family grow closer through all of this, rather than having all of this cause us more problems. When I came back after dinner, Karen was asleep, but soon woke up. Her SATs dropped down to the 60s after she ate again. They were keeping her sedated to rest up for her trip the next day.

The night nurse told me that the day nurse had told her that Corpus had called and said that they had a bed for Karen and would take her the next day. However, there was no specific time set up for the transfer. I prayed for good weather for the next day and thanked the Lord for the available bed. I left Karen's room just before 11:00 and finished reading the book Maura had given me weeks earlier—*Bunnicula*—about a dog, cat, and vampire bunny, written from a dog's point of view. It was a great stress reliever: humorous, absurd, and easy to read, written at a junior high level, which happened to be what Maura taught.

Friday, June 30, was another rainy day. Unfortunately, they didn't have a room for Karen in Corpus after all. Grandma and Maura didn't need to come in the rain to visit as they had planned. I spent my time reading and writing. I had gotten up late, since they had not come to get me, and didn't get to see Karen until 12:30 p.m. She was awake some and cried a little. Most of the time she was quiet, looking around, and chewing on the ventilator tube or licking the tape which held it in place until it came loose. She never seemed to tire of trying to get free from all of this. I went outside for a while and went to the chapel where I prayed, talked to God, and sang a little. I missed praise and worship at church and my praise tapes at home.

Maura came to get me between 6:30 and 7:00 p.m. and took me to the Stables for a steak dinner. I had a filet mignon, baked potato with everything, and salad. Maura had the rib eye. It was wonderful! It beat the hospital food by a long shot. Maura said she hoped that I enjoyed it, because we probably wouldn't do this again for another twenty years. We laughed. Under the circumstances, I hoped it would be at least twenty more until I would need a special meal like that again. We had a chance to talk a long time and didn't get back to the hospital until 9:15. Maura stayed in the room with Karen and me until almost 11:00 p.m. When we first got back, Mom called, and Maura got to tell her "Hi." Maura had been like one of the family for a long time. Dad was doing great, walking a lot. Linda and Phil had visited them earlier and Dad had picked up Angela (their foster child) to carry her to the car. Naturally, Mom told him that he shouldn't have done that. It had been such a peaceful day. What a great change!

On Saturday, July 1, the nurses tried to wake me up in the morning to tell me that Corpus had called to say they had a room. It would be ready in the afternoon, possibly as late as 3:00 or 4:00 p.m., and they would call back with more details. Unfortunately, the nurses couldn't find me because I was in room two, and the night nurse had mistakenly written room three on the parents' board. They had been knocking on the wrong door.

I got up at 10:00, cleaned up, washed my hair, and called PCCU at 11:30 to see if rounds were over, since they were usually earlier on weekends. That was when I found out that we were supposed to go to Corpus that day. Pat and the girls arrived at 12:30, because he had called earlier and found out. At 4:00 p.m. they called to say that the room would not be ready until the next morning. We had all been visiting in Karen's room after we finished lunch in the cafeteria. Frustrated, we decided to go to Grandma Lucy's to wash my clothes, because almost all of them were dirty. Stephanie and I spent some time together by going to K-mart and Payless for toiletries for me and tennis shoes for her. Pat had a chance to rest, and Grandma fixed us sandwiches and melons for a snack. We had a great visit with Grandma, and she gave my husband an unusual Bible translation that had belonged to my Great Uncle Bruce. When we left at 8:00 p.m., we went back to Payless for another pair of tennis shoes for Stephanie and a pair for me, and then got burgers and fries before returning to the hospital. We saw Karen a short time before my husband took the girls to Linda and Phil's. Stephanie was excited because she was going to stay a week and go camping with them Wednesday night. Pat would get someone to help him with Kimi, so that he could get some legal work and housework done and still try to come to see us in Corpus as soon as possible. Karen woke up when we moved her for a chest x-ray, but she was quiet. Her SATs were finally up and in the 90s. I went to the bedroom at 11:00 and to sleep by midnight.

On Sunday, July 2, I woke up at 7:45 a.m. and got out of bed by 8:15. I had finally had my husband bring me a clock so that I could see the time while I was in bed. Corpus had called; the bed wasn't ready yet, maybe later. I cleaned up and went to eat by 10:00. At 10:20 I decided to go to the interfaith worship service at the chapel, and another mother, Cheryl, wanted to go with me. Jack's sermon was about freedom. Pat and Kimi got there at 11:00, just as the service was over. When we went upstairs to see Karen, they told us that the bed in Corpus was ready, and lift off time was set for 1:00 p.m. I was really glad that I had laundered all of my clothes at Grandma's the day before. I called Grandma, Maura,

Claire, and Phil to tell them that we were finally leaving. Then I called Brenda Ross to get her address. I asked Jack to come up to pray for Karen before we left. I could hardly believe that it was really finally about to happen. We weren't ready to leave the hospital until after 2:00 p.m. The ambulance paramedic, the flight nurse (Rose), a respiratory therapist (Steve), and Dr. Young rode in the ambulance with Karen. (Even though she was no longer assigned to PCCU, Dr. Young had requested that she be able to accompany Karen.) One of the Life Flight men took me to the airport in a Hermann Hospital van. It took a lot of time to load the incubator, with Karen inside, and all of the equipment—a neonatal monitor, an oxygen saturation monitor, and some portable oxygen tanks—into the plane. Someone said that the actual flight only took about fifteen minutes, maybe thirty including take off and landing. When I thanked the pilot and copilot, the copilot said that he would be praying for us. I felt so grateful, knowing that there was another person who cared about Karen and would be praying for her.

An Answer to Prayer, or Another Assignment?

But you will receive power when the Holy Spirit comes on you; and you will be my witnesses in Jerusalem, and in all Judea and Samaria, and to the ends of the earth (Acts 1:8 NIV).

An ambulance met us at the Corpus airport. Dr. Young, Rose, Steve, and the ambulance crew rode in the back with Karen and all her equipment, while I sat in front with the driver. We arrived at Driscoll Hospital at 3:45 p.m., but I had to wait until almost 5:00 to see Karen in the Pediatric Intensive Care Unit (PICU). I saw her only a short time before the nurse manager, Larry, helped me register for my parent room, which looked like a hotel room with two twin beds, a nice change from Hermann, where we only had a bed and could not keep anything in the room, and it was on a first-come basis. The disadvantage was that we had to pay for it, but at least I had a place to leave my stuff.

After checking in, I went back to see Karen. Since I heard one of the doctors or nurses talking about getting twenty-seven calorie formula for her to help her gain more weight, I mentioned that I had one bottle of high calorie formula in my room with her other belongings. I went quickly to get her things, but when I got back at 5:40, they said that I couldn't go back in because they were getting a new admission. I had rushed so that Karen could get the formula as soon as possible, but, in return, I didn't get to see her for a while. How discouraging! One of the nurses came out to get Karen's formula and other stuff, and I went downstairs to look for my sister, Cherie, who was coming to visit us.

I stopped to call Mom, my husband, and Grandma and asked Grandma to call Maura, because I was having trouble reaching her. In the lobby, I had the opportunity to meet Dr. Duff, the surgeon, and Dr. Simpson, the cardiologist. They said that they would probably do an echocardiogram the next day, and we would talk more after that. (An echocardiogram obtains an image of the heart structure using ultrasound. Because the sound is reflected differently by each part of the heart, a complex series of echoes results. It is used to detect structural abnormalities of the heart wall [like VSDs] or heart valves and to measure blood flow across valves.)[10]

When I went back upstairs to look for my sister, one of the other moms said that a doctor in intensive care was looking for me. I found Dr. Garcia in PICU, and he asked me questions about Karen's background. Near 7:00 p.m. Cherie got there, and we went to eat *beef'n reef* steak and fried shrimp. I guess there's one **small** advantage to having a very sick child; **Cherie** picked up the tab. When we got back to see Karen after 8:30, she was asleep. She finally woke up and cried some and kept looking for the mobile that had been hanging on her bed at Hermann Hospital. The nurse had also noticed that Karen seemed to realize she was in a different place; she kept looking around and staring at everything. Then the nurse brought out a crib toy that moved and made music and a mirror for Karen to look at and set them inside the crib. Karen settled down a little, but was confused about her surroundings and fretted about the ventilator tube. Cherie and I left PICU at 11:00.

On Monday, July 3, Cherie and I got up late and didn't see Karen until 10:30 a.m. We stayed until noon and then went to Schlotzsky's for a sandwich. After lunch, we went to the Agape bookstore, where I bought more of Hagin's booklets, *Don't Blame God*, because I had given away my others at Hermann. We went back to PICU to see Karen for a while and then went to the gift shop, where I bought Stephanie some slippers and Cherie bought Karen a T-shirt. Cherie really thought that Karen was cute: active, but fairly calm (not agitated) and showing off her personality and temperament. She had never had a chance to come to Lake Jackson to see Karen before that. After we took her suitcases to the car, we returned for Cherie to take pictures of Karen, who was awake and looked like she was pouting. She was sucking on the ventilator tube, but was sticking out her bottom lip. Cherie said that Karen looked like she was watching herself pout in the mirror, and it really did look like it. (Kimi used to watch herself pout and cry in the mirror, to see if she could improve her mournful look.) When Karen was pouting, she had the most sad, pitiful look in her eyes; it almost broke our hearts. Cherie left at 6:20, and my husband arrived with Kimi at 7:00 p.m., and we left right away for seafood dinner. When we got back to the hospital after 8:30, we discovered that John and Kim Haynes had been looking for us, but weren't there then. We took turns visiting Karen and watching Kimi in the lobby.

Dr. Simpson and his patient organizer Cathy explained to us what they would do with Karen. They said that catheterization would be necessary and that banding wouldn't get rid of her VSD problem, but would help with the pressure and extra blood flow (too much fluid) going to her lungs. He explained that banding was basically tightening a pulmonary artery that had just gotten too big from excessive pressure. When they left, Pat brought in the rest of the luggage and looked for John, while I waited with Kimi to see Karen some more. Later, John and Kim came by the lobby and visited with us. The night nurse told us that she would let Kimi into PICU later in the evening if we wanted her to, but we decided that we needed to go to bed early and left by 11:30. Unfortunately, we didn't actually go to bed until after 1:00 a.m.

On Tuesday, July 4, I woke up at 6:00 a.m. to go to the bathroom. I wasn't sure if I had set the alarm or not, but I was too tired to check and figured it probably didn't matter anyway. I woke up again at 7:00 and finally at 8:00 when the alarm went off. I forced myself to get out of bed at 8:15, because Dr. Duff had said that he would probably make rounds at 9:00, and I wanted to be there to learn any information I could about Karen's catheterization scheduled for the next day. When I didn't see him in the lobby by 10:00, I called PICU to go in. Dr. Duff was already there and said that Karen would probably be first and might be scheduled as early as 8:00 a.m. Karen was awake and slightly agitated, so they were getting ready to sedate her. I called Pat to tell him to hurry if he wanted to see her awake. He and Kimi dressed quickly and came to PICU. As soon as we had seen Karen for a short time, we left to get a barbeque sandwich and browse at some neat little antique shops. One was closed, but had unusual dolls in the window and unique gnome and fairy-type characters of plaster and wood with humorous, expressive faces. We needed a break, relief from what was going on at the hospital. Then we found an antique shop that was open and enjoyed looking around. Kimi helped me pick out potpourri bags for her and Stephanie for their bureau drawers. We went back to our room at 1:00, and Kimi and I played that she was a beautiful lady and I was the groom and I picked her from all the other ladies—a long line of them. Then we got married and I put her in a special bed in the back of the car and drove her to our house. Wow! I loved her imagination! She loved to *direct* the whole playtime when possible.

I went back to PICU at 2:00 while Kimi stayed with her dad. When they arrived at 2:30, the nurses were finally ready to let me in. We watched Karen a little while, and then packed the car for Pat and Kimi to leave by 4:30. I tried calling Mom, Grandma, Maura, and John Haynes. I got either a busy signal or a recording to try again; I gave up and went back in to see Karen. I stayed about thirty minutes, went to eat in the cafeteria, then returned to see her for about forty-five more minutes. Sometimes she was sleeping and sometimes she was awake, but she seemed frustrated and sad. The 13-month-old boy beside her screamed loud and occasionally woke her up, and we could tell from the looks she gave us that she didn't like it at all. Karen's SATs fluctuated a lot, between the 70s and low 90s, and she had to get a blood transfusion, because her blood count was low.

I wanted so much to hold her more than just behind her head and neck, but she had too many tubes and monitors connected—a direct ART line (into the artery, to take blood for tests), a direct line into the vein in her right leg (for medicine and the IV), a ventilator tube down her throat (through her mouth; she sucked on it, chewed on it, and slobbered a lot), three small wires connected to monitors on her chest (to check her pulse and blood pressure), another wire on her toe (to check her oxygen saturation), and a continuous feed tube connected to her G-tube (her feeding tube going directly into her stomach). That was a lot of tubes and wires for one small baby! And all of them were in my way and seemed to be keeping me from being a mom!

Karen seemed to like the instrumental tape, "Peace," that I played for her in the morning, but the nurse said that in the evening she liked the mobile music better than the tapes. She was sleeping when I got there at 8:30 p.m. after dinner, but woke up off and on. She still looked so tired and sad.

I read some information from PICU about heart catheterization. Dr. Simpson and Cathy came and explained the risks involved and how he would do the procedure. He said that he had done over 7000 of them and had had few problems, and of those, none were really major. Although Karen might have a higher risk than some, he didn't anticipate any problems. What a refreshing and different perspective from the previous doctors! The catheterization was scheduled for 9:30 a.m. in the x-ray room, because the dye to check the blood flow would show up on the x-ray screen. I signed papers for that. Then he said that if all were okay, they would do the surgery next. It usually took a week of recovery for the patient to go home, but Karen might take longer since she had been on the ventilator so long and had had other problems. They seemed so different from some of the Houston doctors; they seemed to understand our fears and concerns and to care about the children and their parents. I read about Trisomy 18 and 13 in their medical book and looked up some of the terms mentioned in the medical dictionary. When I left the room at 10:30, Karen was asleep.

On Wednesday, July 5, I went to PICU at 9:00 to see Karen before her catheterization at 9:30. They had already sedated her for it. Dr. Simpson said that he needed to go to a clinic for the afternoon and that Dr. Duff would give me the results of what they found out between 3:00 and 4:00 p.m. I went to my room at 1:00 p.m. and called maintenance to adjust the room temperature, so that it wouldn't be so cold. Since they said that they would be up shortly, I lay down to rest and wait. By 1:35 they still weren't there, so I called again, and the girl said that she would check and call me right back. At 1:45 she still hadn't called, so I left a note for them to change the temperature to between 75° and 78°. Restless, I left and walked to the Agape Christian bookstore down the road. It took about fifteen minutes, and they didn't have the books I was looking for, so I bought some Hagin booklets about walking in love and wrong versus right thinking, and *Dr. Dobson Answers Your Questions*.

I then got a fast-food sandwich and got back to the hospital right at 3:00, stopping for a coke before going to PICU. Dr. Duff had just looked in the lobby for me at 3:00. When I found him, he explained the numerical results of Karen's tests on her heart. They felt that the banding would help, so they scheduled the surgery for 2:00 p.m. on Thursday. I stayed in PICU with Karen until about 6:00, took a nap until 8:00, got a chili dog and coke in the snack bar, and went back to see Karen from 8:30 to 10:00. Then I went back to the room and read my new booklets and part of Jeremiah for a while. My husband called to say that he and Kimi would come in the morning near 10:00 to talk to Dr. Duff.

On Thursday, July 6, I got up after 9:00 and went to the snack bar for breakfast. My husband and Kimi got there at 10:30, and we all went up to see Karen. Since the surgery was scheduled for later that day, they let Kimi in PICU to see Karen. The nurses then took a picture of Karen and another one of Kimi, my husband, and me near Karen. While Pat signed the permission paper, they told us that the surgery had been rescheduled for 3:00 or 4:00 p.m. We left for lunch and got back to the hospital just after 2:00. Because they had changed the time back to 2:00, they were already ready to take Karen to surgery, and the operating room nurses were waiting for us. We all rushed in quickly to see Karen before they took her for surgery. By 4:00 p.m. it was over and had gone well. Now we had to see how recovery would go.

Karen had been awake looking around peacefully all morning, looking at the nurses and mobile and mirror, and enjoying our company when we got there. She slept during surgery for about an hour. By 4:30, when we could go in to see her, she was awake again. She looked very uncomfortable, and I'm sure she was. After they gave her morphine and Valium, she finally relaxed some and just slightly moved her head back and forth. We left her after 5:30 to get dinner and to call friends and family to let them know about the surgery and to ask them to pray that she not feel the pain so much, and that she sleep a lot so she could get well. When we got back to the hospital to see Karen, she was sleeping better. We left PICU before 9:30. While Kimi and I read a while, my husband went to bed. At first, Kimi lay on her mat on the floor, then she crawled in bed with me, and finally I put her back on her mat. Pat decided that he and Kimi would stay Friday and the rest of the weekend. I was glad to have the company. Although I did enjoy my husband's company too, Kimi was such a cheerful, positive influence that she was especially fun to have around, the opposite of all the hurt and pain seen in PICU.

Karen was doing much better Friday. She was sleeping peacefully and even smiled a few times, not a big grin, but a quick smile, while she was asleep. It was encouraging to see her so restful—an answer to prayer. We saw her from 10:30 to noon, when we left for lunch and to go to a laundromat to wash my clothes. Although they had brought a few extra clothes, and I wasn't quite down to nothing, I just decided that it was smarter to get them cleaned while we had the car there, instead of having to walk to a laundromat later with a load of clothes.

When we went back to see Karen, she was still sleeping peacefully, so we decided to go to the mall. There was a huge carousel in the middle of the mall; Kimi rode a horse and I rode the carousel on a bench near the horse. We stopped for soup and salad, and then went to a Christian gift shop. Next, we browsed at shoes and clothes, but didn't buy any. However, we couldn't resist the strawberries and cheesecake, which was delicious! Finally, we went back to the hospital to see Karen, who was still doing fine, and we stayed up late again, reading and playing.

On Saturday, July 8, Karen was more awake and a little fussy, but still okay. We saw her from 10:30 to noon, and then went to the Christian Book Shop, where we bought some books, a coloring book and some stickers for Kimi, and a Sandi Patti two-tape package for the girls, in which background music plays while Sandi reads Scriptures and gives a little introduction relating the story to thing kids know about today. Kimi was very impressed and kept telling us to be quiet so she could hear her tape we were playing in the car on the way back. When we returned to the hospital to check on Karen, she was a little fretful, but okay. Since she looked like she was uncomfortable, they gave her a little morphine—the first and only time that day. (She had only had it once Friday also.)

Pat, Kimi, and I decided to go to the beach—Cole Park near downtown Corpus—a man-made beach, because most of the city's coastline is rocky. We had fun playing in the water and sand. Kimi pretended that she was a mother ostrich and made a nest and eggs from the mud, and a small piece of driftwood was the baby ostrich that hatched out of the egg. I was the little girl who ran away from her mother or grandma—Kimi was both of those too—and played with her nest and baby ostrich. My husband was lying beside us on the wet sand (or mud) and couldn't believe what we were playing. As usual, Kimi *directed*. We went back to the room, cleaned up, and went to eat Chinese food. Although it was good, we agreed that Shanghai Restaurant in Lake Jackson was better. When we returned to PICU, Karen was getting only ten respirations per minute from the ventilator, with the oxygen down to 25% or lower, while maintaining SATs in the 80s and 90s. She was doing great!

Pat thought about having us go to the Cathedral of Palms Assembly of God Church near the hospital on Sunday, but since we weren't sure what time the service started, we decided not to go. He got ready quicker and went to see Karen at 10:15, while Kimi and I finished getting ready. We had to recheck the parent room for that night, and then went to PICU to meet him at 11:00. They had taken Karen off the ventilator at 7:30 a.m.—in only three days! So many doctors had suggested that she might be on it for the rest of her life. The nurses said that she was all excited about it at first and peaceful after that. A little later she got cranky, so they gave her something to calm her down.

The nurses enjoyed having Kimi come in to visit Karen. She had drawn a picture earlier one day and asked me to give it to the nurses, but I kept forgetting. Finally Kimi told me to give it to Valerie—the pretty, young, blond respiratory therapist, who accepted it graciously and said that she had a niece who used to draw pictures for her, too. On Sunday, Kimi went in to see Karen again. This time she gave Clare a picture, which she had colored in her Barbie coloring book and had then written her name and Clare's name on it. Clare hung it up on the medicine chest, to Kimi's pure delight!

We left at noon to go to the laundromat to wash jeans, since one pair was a little dirty and the other pair worn over my swimsuit smelled like beach water. We ate hamburgers for lunch, packed their suitcases and stuff into the car, and then went to see Karen again. Kimi gave Connie, another nurse, a colored Barbie picture too and one to Maggie, the mother of Maria Elena, a little three-year-old girl in PICU. Kimi and her dad left by 4:30, while I stayed in with Karen for about an hour. I went to the hospital cafeteria to eat, but because it didn't look too great, I decided to walk to Luby's, about a fifteen-minute walk. I was thinking about getting some fresh cooked broccoli or other vegetables as I passed the Cathedral of Palms Assembly of God Church. Since I noticed a lot of cars and a lot of people going in, I decided to ask someone when church started. I soon changed my mind, because I was never close enough to anyone to ask. As I passed the church, something made me turn around and go back and ask a girl inside what time the service started. She said that it was just starting, so I decided to stay to enjoy praise and worship. Although I recognized the song, when I started to sing, I started crying, just like I had been doing recently during praise and worship at our church. I felt embarrassed, left, and started for Luby's again, deciding I must be hungry after all. When I was barely one or two buildings away, I kept feeling like God was telling me to go back, because he had something there for me. I was sure it wasn't just me thinking it, because I was getting hungry. I finally turned around and went back in. This time I didn't immediately start crying.

The pastor was Sister Gloria. She said that Moses' anointing was given to seventy others, and now her anointing needed to be shared with other church members, who then needed to share the love and other attributes of God with others. Near the end, she made the comment that if we are open, God will use any of us.

While she was praying with people who had gone up front, I suddenly felt a pain in the left side of my chest—about where my heart is. While I was trying to figure out what it was, I felt like God was telling me that I felt it because he was fixing Karen's heart. He was doing something to her heart, and she could feel it, and I could feel it. Just before that, I had started crying, but I didn't feel sad; I just didn't understand what was happening. Excited, I left and went back to the room. Kimi and her dad weren't home in Lake Jackson yet, and no one answered at Family Life Church. I called John's home number, and asked his daughter, Kim, to have Claire call me in the room after 10:00. Then I went back to see Karen. She had been doing well with the oxygen hood at 30% oxygen. When they took her out from under it to suction her and had her on room air only, she still maintained her SATs in the 90s. Dr. Miranda, the resident, then authorized turning her oxygen down to 25%, because they thought that she might be able to come out from under the hood by the next day.

Just after 10:00, I left PICU, in case Claire called me back, but I started talking to Leti's Mom about Karen. (Leti was a beautiful eleven-year-old who was hit by a car, pronounced *dead* at the scene, recovered, and was in a coma.) She asked why we had come here for surgery with all the hospitals in Houston, and I explained it to her. Then I went to my room after 10:30 and called Claire to tell her what had happened at the church. Next, I called Pat and told him what had happened as well as what the nurse had said about Karen's oxygen hood. When I talked with Kimi, she said that she wished that I could come home even if Karen were still sick and had to stay, although she really wished that Karen were well to come home too. I told her that maybe we could both come home soon and then stayed up singing, reading, and writing until 1:15 a.m.

On Monday, July 10, I was tired, had a sinus headache, and had a hard time getting up. I finally got up at 10:00 a.m., because housekeeping needed to change the bed. I cleaned up and went to see Karen, who was slightly fussy, but doing well with the hood. The doctors had decided to leave her under it at least one more day, because she still had some fluid in the bottom of her left lung. After she got some Tylenol, she finally fell asleep. Then the respiratory people woke her up to give her a treatment. She held my finger and fell asleep again, but when I would move my finger to leave, her eyes would open again. We did this two or three times. Finally, I just laid my hand on top of hers, and she barely fell asleep, but I wasn't sure if she was really asleep or not when I left.

I saw Dr. Duff, who said that if her lung continued to clear and she kept doing well under the hood, we might move her to inter-mediate care on the 4th floor the next day. Then I went to eat lunch in the cafeteria and saw the grandma of a little baby girl I had seen in PICU. She told me that her granddaughter might get to go home the next day and sat down to eat with me. I went to the room for a little while, and then back to PICU near 2:30 p.m. Because they were preparing to admit someone new, a boy from the emergency room, we couldn't go in. He had a transplanted kidney and had just had a stroke or heart attack. After they admitted him and got him stable, they life-flighted him out to the Galveston hospital where he had received his transplant. We couldn't go into PICU until after 5:30. By then I had a note waiting for me that my husband had called at 12:20 and had wanted me to call him at work, but it was too late. I stayed with Karen for about an hour. She had just discovered that she could smack her lips and make noise, so she was making funny faces, sticking out her tongue, crossing her eyes, wrinkling up her nose, and smacking her lips. It was great to watch! She was also coughing a lot, which helped to clear out her lungs. The nurse said she was breathing much better than in the morning, now that they had started giving her another medicine (Organidin).

When I went out into the waiting room, I discovered that Leti had gone to surgery to repair her right hand—although she was still in a coma from some swelling on her brain. Leti's mom, Fela, had said that she couldn't forgive her real dad for leaving her mom when they were little, and he had come with his new family to see Leti, but she wouldn't let him. Maggie told me that Fela had also said that she couldn't forgive the lady who hit Leti with her car, even though it was an accident. I asked Maggie if she knew Fela very well, because if she had all that unforgiveness in her, she might not be getting her prayers answered for Leti. Maggie had thought of the same thing, but didn't really know her well enough to talk to her about it. It can be so difficult to deal with all the pain, hurt, anger, and unforgiveness after a child's serious accident or illness, especially with death seeming to wait right there beside them.

I talked to Fela and her husband, John, and her mom, Molly, while they were waiting for Leti's surgery. We talked about kids, Karen, Leti, and a lot of things, while they shared their fried chicken with me. Maggie and her husband had told me earlier that they were going to wash clothes and asked if I needed anything from the store. They bought me the bar of soap I needed. We all seemed to have a special bond, after sharing our lives, our kids, and our feelings. I noticed that they were copying the Scriptures from the booklet I had made at Hermann Hospital into a 3 x 5 spiral note card book in Spanish. It was exciting to see that the idea was spreading.

After we had talked a while, I showed Fela the Scriptures I had written on the 4 x 6 cards in the spiral and asked her if she were reading her Bible aloud to Leti when she read. She was saying her prayers out loud to Leti, but not reading the Bible to her. I read her Proverbs 4:20-22 and Psalm 118:17 and told her that they might help her.

> *My son, give attention to my words; incline your ear to my sayings. Do not let them depart from your sight; keep them in the midst of your heart, for they are life to those who find them, and health to all their whole body* (Prov. 4:20-22 NASB).

> *I shall not die, but live, and declare the works and recount the illustrious acts of the Lord* (Ps. 118:17).

I let her borrow an extra booklet I had made, and a friend of hers copied all the Scriptures down and said that she would write them in a notebook for Fela. Her friend was also telling me about a discipleship class she was taking, and how the teacher told her to write Scriptures in a little purse sized notebook to keep with her to memorize them; these had really helped her reduce her worrying. We had a great time talking until Leti was out of surgery and cleaned up after 9:00, and they went in to see her. I prayed that God would quicken to Fela the Scriptures I had copied into the booklet about praying and unforgiveness hindering answers to prayer (Mark 11:24-26).

I had tried calling my husband for almost an hour until he answered at 8:15. Next I called Stephanie at 9:20 to let her know what was happening here and to see how she was. Then I went in to see Karen. The nurse asked me if I wanted to hold her and couldn't have asked me a better question. She disconnected a few wires to monitors and gave me an oxygen mask to hold close to Karen's face. I was able to rock her for the first time in about a month—from about 9:30 to 10:15. Karen looked at me kind of funny and looked all around at first, like she could hardly believe it. She must have needed it as much as I did. Then she snuggled up and relaxed and made funny faces. Although she almost fell asleep, she woke up right before I put her down. She probably just didn't want to be put back in bed!

I had offered Fela the extra bed in my room the night before, and she had declined. That night she asked me if her Mom could use the bed, since her Mom would be staying to give her a chance to go home for the night. She hadn't spent the night at home since Leti had been admitted. I agreed and told Molly, but later when I went back to PICU after 11:00 p.m., she said that she would stay in the conference room close to PICU, since she had linens and a cot in there. (I saw the linens, but not the cot.) Although I told her to come to the room later if she got uncomfortable, I didn't really expect her to. I finished reading and writing at about 1:20 a.m.—late to bed again!

Tuesday, July 11, was Dad's birthday. I needed to remember to call him. When I went to PICU at 10:00, Karen didn't have her oxygen tent. She was sprawled out with both arms straight out to the side and her legs spread apart. She had freedom of movement for the first time in weeks! She looked so content; she was sleeping great. The nurse asked if I wanted to rock her when she woke up, so I did for about 30 minutes. Several times, they had to wake her up a little, because when she went into a **really** deep sleep, she would hyperventilate and her SATs would go down into the 60s. By afternoon she wasn't doing it anymore, and her SATs stayed in the high 70s to low

80s most of the time, occasionally going higher. By evening they were in the 80s to low 90s most of the time. What a relief!

At 11:00 the nurse needed to take out the ART line in Karen's arm and the central line in her leg to prepare her to go to a room the next day. While she did that, I went downstairs to check out the parent room for one more day. I saw Dr. Duff, who said that the next day we should be able to go to the 4th floor, intermediate care, in a room close to the nurses' station. After Karen's respiratory treatment when I returned, the therapist put her on her back. She threw her right arm across her chest and got it parallel to her left arm, which was sticking straight out. It looked comical, but put her in a position she liked, on her back but a little sideways. Soon she fell asleep. At noon I went to lunch and called Claire to tell her about Karen and to have the prayer chain pray for Maria Elena, Maggie's little girl who was having dye put into her veins to see if enough oxygen was getting through the blood to her brain. They were obviously apprehensive. I called Dad to tell him "Happy Birthday" and to tell him and Mom about Karen. I also gave Kimi's balloons that we had got for her when she was here to Jessica, with the Child Life Department, so that some of the kids she helped could enjoy them.

Karen was still doing well in the afternoon. Her oxygen level was good, but her lungs were a little junky and needed suctioning. At 6:00 I left for dinner and to buy a few miscellaneous items. When I returned to my room, I called my husband and Grandma. I returned to PICU to see Karen from 8:30 to 10:00, but she was sleeping most of the time. We tried to wake her up, rock her, and give her Pedialyte, but she wasn't interested. When I left and went to the lobby, Maggie and Rico wanted to see the spiral Scripture books that I had made just for Karen, to copy some of those too. I brought them from my room, and they copied from them until about 11:30, while I read a book, *Christ the Healer*. Fela's mom, Molly, said that she had seen that book at the HEB and was going to buy it. For then, she just borrowed my Hagin booklet about walking in love, *Love Never Fails*. By reading it, maybe she would be able to explain to Fela about the need for forgiveness. Parents at the hospitals really learned to share what they could with other parents, whether it was books to read, food to eat, prayers, or encouragement. I started organizing my clothes and things for our move to a room the next day and didn't go to bed until after 1:00 a.m. again.

On Wednesday, July 12, I got to PICU right at 10:00 a.m. The other parents were still waiting, and we all went in at once. Karen was asleep, and the nurse finally woke her up so that I could try to give her some Pedialyte by bottle. She made a horrible face—stuck out her tongue, crossed her eyes, and scrunched up her nose and mouth. The nurse said that she had never seen a baby make such a funny, but awful face; Karen obviously did not like the Pedialyte. Next, we tried giving her water. She liked it better, but only wanted one to two cc. of that. I enjoyed getting to rock her anyway.

I left PICU at noon to take my suitcase and other stuff to Room 414W and then went downstairs to turn in the key to the parent room. (414W is the window area of the room.) Next I got a quick lunch in the cafeteria and went back to the PICU lobby at 1:00 p.m. Another family was there speaking Spanish to Fela and to the Trejos when they arrived. I tried in vain to read while all of them were talking in Spanish and laughing. I guess I was a little too curious about what they were saying to be able to concentrate.

Just before 2:00, the nurse came to tell me that they were ready to take Karen to the 4th floor. She had already kicked the IV out of her foot in the morning, and they had left it out the rest of the morning. When Ruth, one of the nurses, tried to put one back in at noon, she and another nurse couldn't get it into Karen's foot. A doctor finally put an IV in her neck, but not a central line this time. They weren't using it for anything, but wanted one for medicine in case of an emergency.

At 3:30 p.m. Karen was wide awake and acting like she might like a bottle. I asked if she could have some water, but the nurses couldn't even get her water then without a doctor's orders. Since Karen had been fussy most of the day and her temperature by 4:00 p.m. was 99.4° axillary (under the arm), or about 100.4° by mouth, I asked then if she could also have some Tylenol. Karen finally got a bottle of five cc. of formula instead of water, and the Tylenol after 5:00. Although I tried for about fifteen to twenty minutes to give her the bottle, she only took about two cc. Apparently, she was out of the mood by then, because she chewed on the nipple more than sucking it. I gave up and left for dinner right before 6:00.

In the lobby I saw Fela, who told me that earlier that morning Leti finally spoke, as she was coming out of her coma. Her mom had asked her if she hurt and she had said, "Yes" twice. In the afternoon they told me that she had said, "Daddy" when they asked her who was there. As you can guess, they were ecstatic!

Karen was doing fine in a room, except for being fussy. She took about another two cc. of formula at 10:00 p.m., but mostly she just chewed or bit on the nipple rather than sucking it. They gave her some more Tylenol around 10:30. Near 11:30 p.m. I lay down to try to sleep, and woke up at 3:30 a.m. when Jim came in to do her respiratory treatment. I heard the nurses come in several times before that, but didn't stay awake for long. Unfortunately, I was also awake off and on between 3:30 and 7:00. What a difficult place to sleep! (I wondered how people could get well in hospitals, because they could hardly ever rest.)

Near 7:00 a.m. on Thursday, July 13, when the respiratory therapist came in and asked what the CO2 monitor read and the nurse said 83, I became wide awake. Actually that was the reading for the SAT monitor, and the CO2 monitor was only about 50. (It should be between 50% and 70%.)[11] I tried to go to back to sleep, but at 7:30 the nurses told me that I needed to move my bed over, because we were getting a roommate. After that I tried, but never went back to sleep. I held Karen for a little while and gave her about two more cc. of formula, but she just didn't seem to remember how to suck any more. It looked like we would need to start her training all over again. After the nurses weighed her, 9 lbs. 4 oz., she went back to sleep. I spoke with Dr. DeLeon, the pediatrician who worked with Dr. Garcia, and then I cleaned up. Dr. Duff came in after that and said that if Karen continued to do so well, we might be able to take her home on Monday. Yes!!! I called Pat to tell him and then went to eat.

Leti was moved to Room 419. She was out of intensive care, too! Her grandma came to borrow a couple more of Hagin's books. She seemed to have an insatiable appetite to learn more and more about the goodness of God.

I was finally getting to rock Karen a lot more, and she and I were both enjoying it. In the evening, Karen was fussy and whiny, like she didn't feel good. I thought that maybe her tummy hurt, because she had gas, needed to go to the bathroom, or was too full. The nurse checked for residual formula in her stomach, but found none. Her tummy wasn't distended either; it was soft. She finally had several small BM's and was still fussy, but she had had a lot of gas with the BM's. At 10:30 I mentioned to the nurses that she was fussier than usual that day, and they gave her a Tylenol suppository at 10:50. She was still fussy at midnight and getting worse, crying louder and harder, so they called the resident, Dr. Wask, a female, who ordered Benadryl for her. She hoped that it would make her a little drowsy and, if the surgery incision hurt or itched, Benadryl would be good for the itchiness. At first I thought it sounded crazy that she would order an antihistamine, that maybe it was just to give Karen something to *please Mom*, but she did have a good reason for her choice. Also, the respiratory therapist ordered a suction catheter and other equipment, suctioned Karen twice within a few hours, and brought up a lot of junk, although she had had a hard time inserting the tube, especially on the right side. Karen finally relaxed a little and went to sleep near 2:30 a.m. Unfortunately, she was awake by 3:30, and the respiratory people came in then too. I didn't get much sleep either.

On Friday, July 14, I slept intermittently until almost 10:00 a.m. Karen was awake when I got out of bed. She was in a better mood and appeared to feel much better; she was looking in the mirror and smiling at herself. When I got excited and told her how pretty she was, she smiled at me, and even grinned really big once or twice. When the respiratory therapist, Juan, came in and said, "Hi," she smiled big at him. (He had been in once earlier, and she seemed to recognize him.) She smiled several more times during the morning and early afternoon. It was such a thrill to see her smile so much again.

Karen looked more peaceful and slept much better Friday than the day before. I had been giving her the medications in her g-tube and had been doing percussions on her chest and back, to help between the respiratory treatments. (Percussions were tapping the body lightly but sharply with an instrument that looked like a rubber donut at the bottom of a bell attached to a handle. Its purpose was to loosen mucus in her lungs.) The nurses and therapists were training me for things I would need to do at home. Karen liked being held and was developing a little whine, either to get held or because she just didn't feel good. Sometimes I wasn't sure which.

I talked to Leti's mom and dad. Leti was doing much better. Maggie's daughter, Maria Elena, was doing better, too. She had started crying a lot for them whenever they weren't there, so they had begun to stay in PICU much more than before; she would wake up more often and could see if they were there or not. Earlier that day, they were even allowed to take her downstairs to the first floor in a wheelchair for a short time. I had checked on the second floor in the late afternoon to see Maggie and Rito earlier, but they had been in PICU with their daughter from 4:00 to 7:00. Fela said that she really knew then that the Lord is good. I realized then that perhaps God had placed me at that hospital to share my faith and trust in the Lord and to help others turn closer to Him.

I was starting to get restless and was having a hard time sitting still in the room by myself when I wasn't rocking Karen. It was even hard to sit and read. I tried sitting in the lobby for a while, but that didn't help. Finally, Karen and I walked around and went to the playroom for a while to look at toys and pictures on the wall. There was a little girl playing in the room who was about two and not much bigger than Karen. She was really cute and had a lot more hair than Karen.

Karen went to sleep at about 9:30 p.m. I got the cot ready and lay down at about 9:45. At 10:20 she woke up, but went back to sleep after 11:00. Then she woke up at 2:30 a.m. and didn't go back to sleep until 4:40. I probably went back to sleep about 5:00 a.m. The rest of the morning was typical, with people in and out, waking us up off and on. Karen took only one cc. of water by mouth twice that day. She still just wasn't interested.

Dr. Pliska, one of Dr. Simpson's associates, said that he had talked with Dr. Allen in Lake Jackson and had made arrangements for us to go home Monday and be back in his care. We would need to get the continual feed equipment after we were home. I was so glad that we would finally be going home after over six weeks!

I was pleased, too, that they were working so close with Dr. Allen. At Hermann, the staff had kept in touch with him for the first week or two, but failed to keep him informed of Karen's condition after that. I had not realized this until I spoke with Carlotta later, and she told me that her dad was afraid that the doctors or other staff might be using Karen as a *guinea pig*, because of her genetic condition. After all, they were connected with a medical school for the students to gain as much knowledge about various diseases and treatments as they could from their patients. It hurt him to think that they might be treating her as a condition or a statistic, rather than the individual little baby who she was.

On Saturday, July 15, I got up between 9:00 and 9:30 a.m. Karen was awake and slightly fussy. When she went back to sleep, I cleaned up. Then I gave her a bath when she woke up, and she was really fretful, being mindful to let me know she didn't like the idea of a bath at all. While I rocked her back to sleep, the nurse or aide changed her bed.

Dr. Carlson confirmed Monday's arrangements, and said that Karen's lungs sounded clear and she was doing fine. The brain scan they had done while she was in PICU before surgery had not shown any abnormalities. He reminded me to continue working with her feeding, but cautioned me not to be surprised if she could never eat all of her food by mouth. He also mentioned that I would need to be careful giving her antihistamines for her stuffy nose, because some have a stimulant which would make her heart beat faster, and also keep her awake more. Otherwise, they would be fine to give for her nose.

I went to eat, and just as I walked back into the room, my husband called. Because he hadn't gotten a good night's sleep like he had planned, he was still getting ready. He probably wouldn't leave until 3:00 or 4:00, and wanted to know where he could stay when he got there. I told him that he might be able to stay on a couch or in a parent room, if there were one available. Then he surprised me by replying that he would probably get a motel room instead, or wait until the next day.

I was getting extremely frustrated at his indecision, especially his wanting me to try to get him a room, but not knowing if he would come that night of if he would even stay in the room if he did. He finally said that he would call back in 30 minutes, but he didn't.

When Karen woke up, I rocked her back to sleep after Sylvia did cardiopulmonary therapy (CPT) on her. Sylvia and I talked about our children, and she said that she would be back at 4:00. After 4:00 Karen went to sleep, and I walked to HEB and Winn's. I looked for a gift for Kimi and bought some odds and ends and some food for dinner. Next, I went to the second floor to talk to Maggie and Rito and get their address and phone number. I waited awhile in PICU to talk to Teri Norris, one of the nurse supervisors, but when she wasn't back by 5:50, I went back upstairs to see Karen. She was awake, but not fussing. That was a great change!

On the fourth floor, I saw Teri talking to some nurses. I showed her the extra spiral book of Scriptures and asked her if she would be able to use it for other parents in PICU. I mentioned that Leti's and Maria's parents had written out the Scriptures too, and Maggie and Rito had done them in Spanish, which might be good to have at this hospital, since many of the patients were Hispanic. A neonatal nurse was with her and asked her if she could use the book in her area too. I mentioned that the head chaplain at Hermann Hospital had talked about copying the pages and stapling them together, because that would be easier. Teri then said that Doris Alvarez, one of the social workers, could probably translate the verses into Spanish. I was glad she was interested and would be able to use the Scripture booklet.

Karen woke up and was smiling again, and grinning too. Since she was in such a good mood, I tried giving her the bottle again. She smacked and made noises with her tongue and grinned, but wasn't very interested in drinking her bottle. However, she did get about three to four good sucks with her mouth closed around the nipple, which was quite an accomplishment. I told her how big she was and didn't try to push her to do anymore for a while. After about five to ten minutes I tried again, but she didn't want it, so we quit. We had done a lot that day, just having her grin, smack, and suck again.

I rocked Karen back to sleep and then started my dinner. Before I was through, she woke up, so I rocked her back to sleep. I finally ate the rest of my dinner at 9:30 p.m. and was hoping to go to bed then. Unfortunately, she woke up. After I rocked her a long time and put her back in bed, I'm not sure when I finally went to bed, totally exhausted.

On Sunday, July 16, I started to get up before 9:00, but then lay back down and didn't get up until almost 11:00. People had been waking us both, or Karen had been waking me up off and on all morning as well as night, and I was exhausted. When I got up, I showered and dressed and then bathed Karen when she woke up.

My husband finally arrived at 2:00 p.m. We went out for lunch and then went back to the room and talked awhile. Leaving him with Karen, I went to HEB for laundry soap, to Winn's for another little gift for Kimi, and to the laundromat. I had hoped to be back by 6:00 to go to the Assembly of God Church a few buildings down from the hospital again, but didn't return to the hospital until 6:35. Neither Pat nor I wanted to go alone and leave the other one, but he reminded me that our pastor had suggested that we tell the pastor there about what had happened the previous Sunday, whether we told her in person or wrote her when we returned home. I knew that it would be easier to go then than to write when I was back home with Karen, so I went to church at about 7:00 p.m. She was still preaching and had persuaded almost everyone to come forward to commit their lives to God to use them for His service. After the service, I told her about the previous Sunday and told her that if her church was looking for a ministry, the Children's Hospital desperately needed one there. There were many moms and dads there just looking for answers—about their children's illnesses, about life, about death, and about God's involvement in it all. I also told her that I had left a 4x6 spiral book of Scriptures with the nurse supervisor, Teri, who was probably going to get the verses translated into Spanish, since so many patients were Hispanic. I suggested that she might want to contact Teri. That would give her church members a good tool to work with or get started with, and they could take it from there. She thanked me and told me that she would give our testimony in church later.

When I returned to the room at 9:00, Pat and I went out for a hamburger. I tried to sleep between 10:00 and midnight, but he kept asking me questions or a nurse or respiratory therapist (RT) would come in and ask questions. Then my husband asked the nurses on the second floor if he could sleep on the cot in the conference room near PICU. After he had rocked Karen and put her to sleep at midnight, he went to the second floor to sleep. I was really annoyed that he had kept me up when I tried to sleep, and had then gone somewhere else to make sure that he could sleep. Karen woke up at 3:00 and went back to sleep. Then she woke up at 4:00, and I rocked her until 5:00. She woke up again at 6:45, when a nurse or RT came in, and went back to sleep. At 7:45 our roommate started watching Sesame Street and that really woke me up. At 8:30, Pat came in and started rocking Karen. I hoped he had slept, since he had to drive home, because I certainly hadn't. I was still trying to decide how and where to get some sleep.

We cleaned up, ate breakfast, got all our belongings ready for our trip home, and talked with the doctors and nurses about all the preparations we would need to make when we returned to Lake Jackson. First, we would need to contact Dr. Allen to let him know that we were back, then call a medical supply company to rent a feeding pump, and finally fill all of her prescriptions for medicine. The nurses took Polaroid pictures of us with Karen when she was dressed and ready to go. We signed all of the necessary papers for release, talked with Dr. Duff and thanked him for his help and concern for Karen as a baby, and we were finally ready to go. After the long trip home, we could sit back and relax and be *normal* again, whatever that is.

Our Little Angel

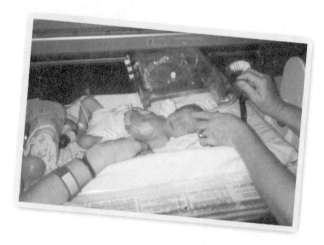

Karen in the incubator before leaving
Hermann Hospital on December 24, 1988.
Karen didn't feel well at all, but liked
Mom's touch and holding her finger.

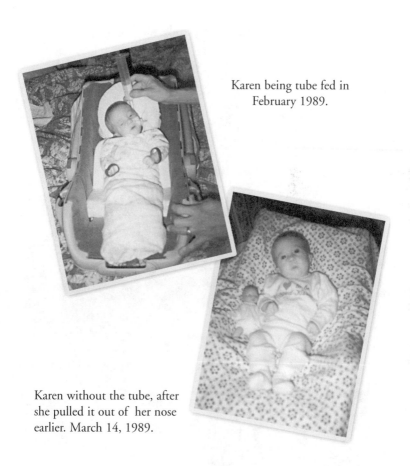

Karen being tube fed in
February 1989.

Karen without the tube, after
she pulled it out of her nose
earlier. March 14, 1989.

Karen on her four month
birthday. Is the jig
an appropriate dance
for birthdays?

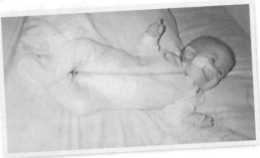

Karen learned to grin
on May 1, 1989,
and thoroughly enjoyed
doing it for all.

Karen liked to touch someone
or something when she went
to sleep. May, 1989

Karen and sisters,
Stephanie and Kimi

Karen with ventilator
tube down her throat,
breathing for her.
June 22, 1989

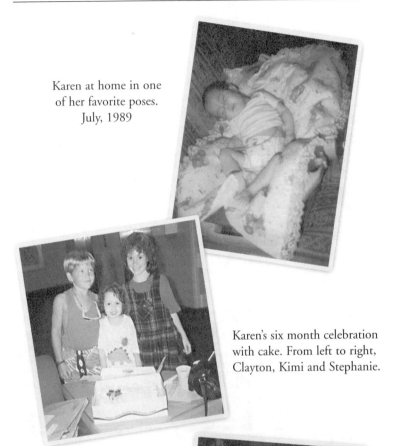

Karen at home in one of her favorite poses. July, 1989

Karen's six month celebration with cake. From left to right, Clayton, Kimi and Stephanie.

Karen and Mom enjoying a special moment.

Kimi and Karen were best friends as well as sisters—very comfortable with each other, even with feeding tubes and pumps. August, 1989

Kimi "reads" from memory one of her favorite books, *God Made Me Special.* August, 1989

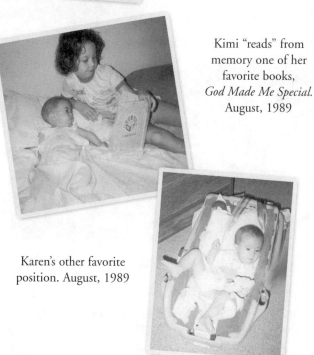

Karen's other favorite position. August, 1989

Karen in Mom's lap, smiling at her sisters standing on either side of Mom. September, 1989.

Karen didn't want her picture taken and made it obvious! Looks like "Na na na na na!"

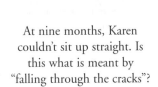

At nine months, Karen couldn't sit up straight. Is this what is meant by "falling through the cracks"?

At ten months, Karen sits
much better without support.
October, 1989.

Kimi and Karen after our trip
to the cardiologist in Victoria
on November 7, 1989. Karen
had been running a fever for
most of the afternoon and
did not feel well at all.

Karen after she had learned to hold toys for more than a few seconds. She could now pick them up and hold them for several minutes. This was her last photo. December, 1989.

After Karen's funeral, Kimi started asking for snow on Christmas (a near impossibility in Lake Jackson). Still, Kimi prayed. On December 22, 1989, Karen's birthday, it snowed. Karen's birthday present to us!

Sleeping in about the same
position she used to sleep in here,
our little angel was home.

119

CHAPTER TEN

Home

The day was Sunday, July 17, 1989. It was strange to be home again after over six weeks of hospital life, really home again, with Karen. In reality, it was anything but normal life with a baby girl. The first things we needed to do were to get her heart medication prescriptions filled and to rent a feeding pump and the bags in which to put her formula. To keep up with all the changes, my life seemed to rotate around a notebook in which it was necessary to keep track of all of Karen's medicines, vitamins, and the times we replaced her empty feeding bags. Since I had previously needed to set my alarm to get up and feed her by syringe and tube every three hours, the feeding pump was a timesaver (or sleep saver) for me. Except for the Tylenol, which she had to have every four to six hours as needed for fevers, (a common problem after heart surgery), every eight hours was the most frequent interval for her new medicines. (Dr. Simpson explained to me near the end of July that the pericardium, the membranous sac enclosing the heart, could get inflamed after surgery, causing the fever.)

Karen woke up frequently too, as babies often do, for routine diaper changes or for being held or rocked, but at least I was getting a little more sleep. I began keeping track of her higher temperatures, as well as when I gave her medicines and vitamins, changed her feeding bag, gave her Pedialyte from a bottle, or occasionally fed her with a syringe when going somewhere or disconnecting the feeding pump and moving her to another room. That was a *routine* day. If I hadn't written it all down, there was no way that I would have ever remembered when I did what, especially on the days I didn't get much sleep.

Not only did she frequently have a fever, but she had also begun to spit up and throw up a lot more than before the surgeries. One of our **best** mistakes at home was the day her pump somehow got disconnected from her gastrostomy tube (G-tube) and poured formula all over the bed during the early morning hours while we slept. What a joy and a jolt to wake up to!

On August 1, we took Karen to the doctor's office for a checkup. By then her weight was 9 lb. 4 oz., not great for a baby $7^1/_2$ months old, but good for Karen. There we gave her 10 cc of Pedialyte by bottle, in one hour. Later, she took 20 cc. from a bottle in two hours. Then we went to the hospital for her complete blood count (C.B.C.). I assumed the C.B.C. was to check for any other possible cause for her fevers besides the heart surgery. Her white blood cell count was near 15,000, which they told me was a little high, but okay. (A normal count is 5,000 to 10,000 per cubic millimeter.)[12] Two weeks later, after I had given her a sponge bath, she drank over 20 cc. in about 15 minutes. I think that was a record, because it usually took one to two hours for her to drink 10 to 20 cc., with the aim of about 40 cc. per day. Because her hard palate was very high and her soft palate was short at the back of her mouth, it was more difficult for her to suck than it was for most babies. That was probably what also accounted for her lack of normal baby cooing sounds; most of her sounds were guttural or throaty, except for her usual weak cry.

On August 4, there was a little blood around the top part of her G-tube, but it stopped oozing and dried up within a few hours. Several weeks later, when I gave her formula with a syringe, she started gagging and spitting up and it looked like there were partially digested flecks of brown in the spit-up formula, perhaps from dried blood from the sore area around the place her G-tube went in. Shortly after noon that day she started to spit up again and got some in her nose, which I suctioned out. I picked her up and held her in my arms, thinking that maybe part of the trouble was the large volume of food she was getting while lying down, even though she was propped up a little on my pillow. Another problem she was having then was her stuffy nose. I propped her up with an extra pillow, but by the last 10 to 20 cc. she started to choke again. A few minutes later, she had a **very** messy diaper. Maybe she was just too full! She seemed to do fine the next day, but the following day she started choking again when we were giving her formula through a syringe. That time it started backing up through her tube, again showing brown flecks and pieces like dried blood in her partially digested formula. After then, we didn't see any more brown flecks, but we were never quite sure what caused it.

There were other changes for Karen too. Near the first of August, she was on her tummy watching her hand and fingers move in front of her face. She may have finally realized that she had some control over making them move. She seemed intrigued.

On August 21, Dr. Allen told us to finish giving Karen the 24 and 27-calorie formula we had received from the hospital and then switch her to Similac with iron. Otherwise, it would cost us about $50 per week to special order the 24-calorie formula. A few days later I tried giving her 10 cc. of formula by bottle and the rest through her tube, just to see if she could do it. Although we usually gave her only water or Pedialyte in the bottle, to my surprise she did just fine. On September 7, Dr. Allen said that we could then start her on rice cereal, but we didn't right away. She was progressing slowly, but she was progressing nonetheless. I was so thankful.

By Monday, September 11, she had a lot of drainage, more coughing, wheezing, and harder breathing. We added Triaminic (a decongestant) and Augmentin (an antibiotic) to her list of medicines, and her doctor told us not to give her Tylenol unless her fever was 102° or higher, to give her body a chance to fight the infection as much as possible. By the 16th, she started screaming and crying and her tummy seemed extremely taut. Apparently she was constipated, because the suppository he told us to give her worked wonders, easing her pain and making her feel much better. I wondered if the medicines could have messed up her already sensitive system. Normally, however, antibiotics would cause diarrhea, not constipation. On Sunday, when Karen was ill again, another doctor was on call, and suggested some Benylin expectorant or Tussy Organidin (another cough remedy) and advised us to stop the Triaminic. Karen had been coughing a lot and crying when she coughed, like it either hurt or she couldn't cough up the stuff, or both. On Wednesday she had a hard knot on the right side of her tummy, about halfway between her belly button and her groin. We gave her another suppository, but it took several days for it to work.

On Friday, she slept from 6:00 a.m. until noon, six straight hours. I believe that might have been a record for her. That day she also started crying because of constipation again. Dr. Allen had us add Karo to each feeding bag of formula and hold off on giving her cereal until later. On September 14, we had to take Karen to the South Texas Pediatric Cardiology Associates clinic in Victoria, Texas for her two-month checkup after surgery to see Dr. Simpson and his associate, Dr. Pliska. They said that she seemed to be doing fine, considering all the problems she had, and her post-operative condition was stable. Her weight then was 10 lb. 6 oz. and her height was 24 inches.

A friend of ours, Maricel Maschmeyer, volunteered to drive us there and back, a three-hour trip each way, so that I could sit in the back with Karen to feed her and take care of her if she cried or spit up or choked. I would have been a wreck trying to drive if Karen had started crying in the back seat or if I had heard her start choking. Kimi went with us, sometimes riding in the back with Karen and me and sometimes in the front. After our office visit, we went out to eat. While there, I fed Karen using a syringe. A lady at the restaurant came over to us and said that she couldn't help but see that we fed Karen through her G-tube. She then asked if we would mind if she prayed for Karen. That was an offer I couldn't refuse.

That incident reminded me of a story that Mother had told me earlier about an acquaintance in one of her political organizations. This person was telling Mom that she had been visiting family one of the previous weekends and had gone to church with them. While there, the church body had prayed for a baby girl who was very ill. As my mom began to ask the lady for more details about the child and where the church was, you can imagine the lady's surprise and Mom's shock when Mom told her, "That's my granddaughter!" I guess it's not only a small world, but God seemed to have prayer warriors for Karen all over the state, and who knows where else.

On September 30, her formula spilled all over the bed again during the night. What a fun way to wake up! On Sunday, October 1, we took her for a short time to our annual church picnic at one of the parks. Later that day we could feel hard places in her distended tummy, and she had also begun to cry; time for another suppository. The next day she cried and whined all morning. On Tuesday she seemed better, but by Thursday we took her to Dr. Allen for a checkup. We increased the Karo and decreased the Tylenol, which can cause constipation, giving it only if the fever was 101.5 or higher.

On Saturday, October 7, Carlotta, Dr. Allen's daughter and office manager and my friend, kept Karen while we had a birthday party for Kimi. A few other times our neighbors down the street had kept Karen, so that we could go out either to see a movie or to go to a meeting. The husband, Donny, had previously been an emergency technician and Mary was a mother who loved to hold and rock babies. Even a few women from our church had come to the house to hold and rock Karen, simply to let me have a much-needed hour or two of rest. It was so helpful to have a few caring people who could help us with her.

About a week and a half later, after another suppository and the hoped-for results, Karen seemed to be feeling much better. She felt so much better that she even started grinning and laughing a lot afterwards, even laughing out loud, a real rarity! On Saturday, October 21, Karen started wheezing in the afternoon. The same doctor was on call as before, and he advised us to stop Triaminic and started Karen on Proventil (a bronchodilator which widens the airways in the lungs) and Ceclor (another antibiotic), as well as the Organidin and other medicines she took regularly. (I was a little concerned about the Proventil, because it could cause the heart to beat harder or faster.) On Monday, we took her back to Dr. Allen, who said to give her Triaminic too. This time she was so plugged up that she was not only fussy, but they could hardly take her rectal temperature. She had to get a suppository first. What fun for the nurse, who fortunately for us was Dr. Allen's wife, an understanding and compassionate woman, who didn't seem to mind the inconvenience too much. A couple weeks later Dr. Allen said to use Organidin only if she coughed and Proventil only if she wheezed.

On October 24, I contacted the Brazoria County Association for Citizens with Handicaps (BACH) Rehabilitation Center, because Dr. Aceves had suggested that we get some form of infant stimulation for Karen. They had an Early Childhood Intervention

(ECI) clinic in Lake Jackson. Dr. Allen had not recommended any such program yet, probably because of Karen's low immunity and high susceptibility to any infections, which would make it necessary to do the therapies and screenings at home.

At an initial visit on October 26, I filled out a lot of papers for them to get medical information from Karen's various doctors. Dr. Allen's statement to them included the following: "Her diagnosis is Trisomy 18 with Congenital Heart Disease (a heart abnormality that has been present since birth). She is growth, developmental, and mentally retarded." On November 9, Jeri Bearden, a caseworker with BACH; Sara Rhodes, the lead therapist; and Judy Griffin, a physical therapist, came to our house and began the screening and TEAM evaluation of Karen. At that time, Karen could roll in both directions and was scooting and trying to crawl. She would reach for toys, but wouldn't hold them. We told them that we normally limited her bottle to water, because of her tendency to aspirate. They observed that her soft palate was short and her tongue was uncoordinated, which would account for her swallowing and sucking difficulties. They also set up a schedule for a monthly monitor for physical and occupational therapy and told us how to follow a home program in between times.

Their evaluation included:

Posture

Lying on her back: "Karen can hold her head in midline but prefers to keep the head to one side. Hands are usually fisted," bent in at the wrist, and legs are bent.

Lying on her tummy: "Karen can turn her head from side to side but is unable to lift head to 45°." Arms aren't in line with the body and legs are extended.

Sitting: "Head and trunk control is poor."

Gross Motor: "Karen is at a two month level in gross motor activities. She has poor head control and no trunk control."

Fine Motor: "Karen is at the one-to-two month level in fine motor/visual motor skills. She will visually track horizontally past midline, upwards and downwards. She does not track 180°. She brings her hands to midline and keeps her hands open 50% of the time. Karen does not move her arms at the sight of a toy or actively grasp a toy. She can maintain grasp on a toy that is placed in her hand for approximately one minute, but her grasp appears more reflexive than intentional. Karen frequently holds her hands in an unusual posture, with fourth and fifth fingers flexed and index finger extended, which is typical of the syndrome."

Self-Help/Oral Motor Development: "...She has an abnormally high palate... "

Speech and Language: "Karen has a weak cry which is typical of her syndrome. She cries in response to distress or discomfort. No other sounds are noted."

Social-Emotional (Behavior): "Karen established eye contact and will occasionally smile at her family when played with. Her mother reports that Karen will visually attend to her five-year-old sister and appears to enjoy being held. Her mother also reports that Karen imitates sticking out her tongue. She is at the one- to three-month level in social skills."

Summary: "Karen is severely delayed in all developmental areas. At 11 months of age, she is functioning at the one- to three-month developmental level. Her greatest strengths are her social skills, which include her ability to respond to her family by smiling or quieting, etc. Her greatest weaknesses seem to be her motor skills. Her functional abilities fluctuate due to her frequent spiking fevers and respiratory problems. Her family is very concerned and [they] appear to be providing Karen the best possible care and a warm and loving environment. Due to Karen's medical problems, direct therapy will be limited to twice a month. Emphasis of therapy will be teaching the family to carry out the home program."

Her physical and occupational therapy goals were to improve gross motor development, improve fine motor development, and to facilitate social/cognitive and language development. The caseworker's goals were to act in an advisory role, consult with the parents, and give general support.

On November 3, we gave Karen her first rice cereal, very watered down. As expected, she didn't like it any more than most other babies do their first time. She didn't take much, but she made lots of funny faces over it, sticking out her tongue and squinching up the rest of her face.

On November 7, we took Karen back to Dr. Simpson's clinic in Victoria. By then she was 11 lb. 10 oz. and 26 inches long. While we were there, her fever went up to 104.2° in the waiting room, and after we finally were able to check with the doctors, we gave her some Tylenol, bringing her fever down to 103.7° by 5:50 p.m. That evening when we took a picture of her and Kimi, she looked like she really didn't feel well. She still had a fever, but at least it was down to 101.8 by 10:00 p.m.

The next day, Wednesday, November 8, we took her to Dr. Allen, who ordered her a shot of Ampicillin. Her fever was back up to 103.1° at 3:00 p.m., 103.6 at 6:00, and down to 101.9° at 9:40. On Thursday, she had diarrhea, once so bad that it went all over the bed. We finally called Carlotta (after hours), who told us not to add any more Karo to the formula and to watch the texture of her bowels, adding the Karo back as soon as possible. Unfortunately, she had the same problem the rest of the day and Friday also. By Monday, November 13, I was finally able to start adding the Karo back to her formula. She was fussy all day, especially at bedtime. By Tuesday her bowels were watery again and finally back to diarrhea. We decreased the Karo, but by then it was too late. I decided to try to give her cereal again to see if that would help, but she was still not impressed. We continued trying to regulate her bowels with the amount of Karo added to her formula. However, by late Thursday, she also had a lot of gas, and Friday morning she fussed a lot. I was getting so frustrated trying to determine what and how much to feed her and to distinguish between symptoms and causes of all of her digestive problems.

On November 16, Sara Rhodes from BACH came out and continued their evaluation. That day Karen tracked vertically and horizontally, but not 180°. When positioned on her elbows, she held her head up briefly, but became very agitated. No reflexes were noted. There was increased tone in her upper extremities, and her fingers curled in a strange pattern (as they usually did). Karen appeared to imitate sticking out her tongue. Her weight was 11 lb. 6 oz. Within a week, Karen had started crying a lot and putting her fingers in her mouth. I wondered if she had begun teething, or just didn't feel well, because her chest was congested too.

On November 22, the people from BACH called us and set up an Individualized Family Service Plan (IFSP). The annual goal was: "TEAM aid in family functioning related to family's and child's strengths and needs." They assessed that our family strengths were our concern and love for Karen and our willingness to work with her. Karen's strength was her determination. Our family needs were input from the therapists on what to do for home activities and time allocation for Mom; in other words, helping me find the time to do the home therapy program with

Karen. Karen's needs were to become as mobile as possible, to be able to eat orally, to make sounds, and to be able to hold objects (other than toys or people's extremities or clothes). They knew that I realized that these were long-term needs. Their number one goal was to improve Karen's independence. The other goals and objectives for Karen were head control and rolling (physical therapy) and grasping and improved tracking (occupational therapy). The family goal was open communication. Our priorities were greater mobility and increased oral feeding.

Thursday, November 23 was Thanksgiving. We were stressed, but thankful that Karen had made it to 11 months the day before. One more month and she would be one year old, beating the odds. It was not a good day otherwise; it got off to a very bad start. Stephanie was up early to go to her dad's and Kimi was also up to go with Bami to her grandfather's. I made a comment to Stephanie about not stretching her nightshirt over her knees, which were pulled up to her chest. It wasn't a big deal to me, just a suggestion, but apparently my husband, who was stressed, decided that it was a good time to enforce strict obedience. That one comment eventually escalated into a terrible display of anger, with yelling, kicking, and throwing things, and eventually hysterics too, all witnessed by two wide-eyed little girls. I was emotionally wounded, but I ached for them more, thankful though that they would be going somewhere else to have fun with other people who loved them. Only much later that evening did I even consider and finally prepare a quick chicken dinner.

On Saturday, November 25, my husband watched Karen in the late morning to early afternoon while I napped and then went to the store. It was good to be out by myself, because I wasn't allowed that privilege very often. On Sunday, she kept waking up every 30 minutes to one hour, probably because of her teeth. She cried and fussed and wouldn't go back to sleep for a long time.

Then she spit up after choking on mucus. What fun! Tuesday, November 28, she fussed and griped and cried almost all night. On Wednesday, I tried to give her more cereal when the ladies from BACH were there, so they could see how she did. Then her bowels started getting hard again, so I had to increase Karo again until they were back to normal. Saturday and Sunday it went from severe constipation to diarrhea. How was I to keep it regulated or normal? It was really discouraging. I went from Karo to cereal to suppositories to nothing and back again.

On Tuesday, December 5, Judy Griffin, a therapist with BACH, came to our home and discussed the home program with me. At that time, when Karen was on her tummy, leaning over a towel rolled up under her chest, she was able to push up on her hands. That progress was unfortunately followed by more fussy days. Then from Saturday through the next Friday, her fever frequently went up to past 102° and 103°, to as high as 103.9° by Friday, December 8.

On Sunday, December 10, at 9:30 p.m., Kimi was lying beside Karen on Kimi's bed. When she put her arm around her baby sister and barely touched the tummy area, Karen's gastrostomy tube popped out, spewing formula up and out. We all freaked out at first, but then I remembered that Sally had warned me that the tubes could eventually come out and would usually close up quickly, somewhat like a newly pierced ear when the earring comes out and stays out for very long. I asked someone to quickly run to the bathroom for some towels to put over the wound, or hole, to sop up the formula squirting out. Within about five minutes, the hole did almost close up, with just a little food seeping out occasionally. We rushed Karen to the emergency room to have them insert a #14 foley catheter. We had to call Sally or Dr. Aceves to get the particulars on the type of catheter for an infant and the procedure to install it, because the staff at our hospital wasn't familiar with it. We were home by 11:30 p.m. and were feeding her again. Unfortunately, her new catheter didn't adapt to the syringes or feeding pump as well as the G-tube had. Some of the food squirted out when we tried to feed her. On Tuesday I had to clean the area around the new tube. She cried and whined like it really hurt. The catheter also moved around, slipping a little in and out, so that I was afraid that it might eventually puncture something or get pulled out.

We talked to the University of Texas Medical School Pediatric Clinic in Houston about our various options for Karen, since she was then scooting and trying to crawl when on her tummy. On Wednesday morning, December 13, we took Karen to Houston to the clinic. Dr. Andrassy replaced Karen's temporary catheter with a *button*, a gastrostomy device that would lie against the skin, rather than having a tube hanging down. Then we went to Grandma Lucy's in southwest Houston, for a nice long visit. She got to hold Karen and rock her and sing to her. We all loved it. That afternoon and evening we gave Karen Tylenol for the pain, as the nurse had instructed us to do.

The *button* was made of biocompatible silicone material that lies flat against the skin, with a plug attached by a snap ring to provide secure closure when the person is not feeding. A catheter adapter was provided to use with a feeding pump. The instructions said to be sure to push the adapter in as far as it could go. Unfortunately, early the next morning we must not have pushed it in far enough, because the tube from the feeding pump came out of her button and the formula went all over the couch. We had done it again!

At 2:00 a.m. on December 14, Karen's fever was 103.4° and by 7:00 a.m. it went up to 106.2°. We gave her Tylenol and sponged her off to reduce the fever and called Carlotta. We made an early appointment with Dr. Allen and got her there as soon as the office was open. By then her fever was 105°. It was pneumonia again, so we had to rush her to the hospital. There they put her on a nasal cannula for oxygen. Since they couldn't get an IV into her any place, it was a good thing that she had the gastrostomy, so she could get fed and not dehydrate. They gave her the antibiotics by injection. By Friday night she seemed much better, and we thought that we might take her home soon. The nurses told me to try to get some sleep. I was so tired; I definitely needed the rest. I relaxed a little and was looking forward to taking her home again.

CHAPTER ELEVEN

Miracles

There is a time for everything, and a season for every activity under heaven... a time to be born... and a time to heal... a time to weep and a time to laugh... a time to be silent and a time to speak, a time to love... (Eccl. 3:1-8 NIV).

We repeatedly saw many answers to prayer and miracles in Karen's life, not *big* miracles, but the little ones often unnoticed and unappreciated. At two days old, she got pneumonia, and her doctor wasn't sure that she would make it, but she recovered and was back in Lake Jackson in only five days.

Again, I remember looking at her at about three weeks old and suddenly realizing that she had muscles in her legs for the first time. I mentioned this to one of the nurses, who said that they had noticed it too. We weren't surprised, though, since Karen was always kicking her legs and moving her arms while she fussed and made pouty faces about the *room service* she was getting. Inadvertently, she was giving herself the exercise she needed to develop those muscles. We also had asked our prayer chain to pray that she develop muscle tone in her arms and legs, because, according to statistics, Trisomy-18 babies should not have good muscle tone, if any muscles or muscle tone at all. But Karen did!

She grew and was finally big enough to leave the hospital, although she couldn't take a bottle or nurse, but she had made it past her first month. Most *Trisomy-18* babies don't live past their first month. We learned how to tube feed her and watched her grow.

On June 1, 1989 Karen got pneumonia again and had to be flown by helicopter to Hermann Hospital. Since she recovered from the pneumonia quickly, we decided to have a gastrostomy tube put into her stomach for feeding, to see if that would reduce the nasal irritation from the feeding tubes. She healed quickly from surgery, but got another high fever, either pneumonia again or congestive heart failure, depending on whom I asked and when I asked. (Congestive heart failure is the inability of the heart to keep up its workload of pumping blood to the lungs and the rest of the body. Left-sided failure can cause the left side of the heart to increase in size and the muscular walls to thicken and can cause an increase in the heart rate. The left side doesn't completely empty with each contraction or has difficulty accepting blood returning from the lungs. A back pressure is created and the lungs become congested with blood. The main symptom is shortness of breath, sometimes causing the person to awaken at night with breathlessness, wheezing, or sweating. Right-sided failure can be caused from left-sided failure or other abnormalities like septal defects. This can lead to an enlarged liver or congestion of the intestines. Both can be treated with drugs and/or surgery. Through hindsight and a lot of reading, I realize that Karen had many of these problems, but I didn't know then that they were related to her heart defects.)[13]Again, she recovered and was taken off the ventilator.

Early one morning, Karen's heart stopped beating correctly and fibrillated (or quivered) instead, not once but twice. The chaplain awakened me at approximately 4:00 a.m. to tell me the bad news, and the doctor later came out of pediatric intensive care and told us that Karen was okay then. Her heart was beating regularly again, but she needed to stay on the ventilator, at least temporarily. One of the nurses later told me that they had not even had to shock her heart to get it to beat again; it had started by itself both times. The nurse had never seen that happen before; shock treatment had always been necessary for other patients she had seen.

Karen had a large hole in her heart that needed repair, because it caused too much blood (fluid) to go to her lungs. That caused her low oxygenation and breathing problems, which then caused her heart to beat too fast. It was a vicious cycle; death would eventually result if no one would or could repair her heart. Texas Children's Hospital wouldn't operate since they felt "Trisomy 18 is lethal anyway." Dr. Simpson and Dr. Duff at Driscoll Hospital in Corpus Christi were willing to do banding on Karen's pulmonary artery, and the surgery had a positive effect on her heart. She even recovered and healed quickly.

Although the doctors in Houston and Corpus Christi had said that Karen might never be able to come off the ventilator, she was off the ventilator in three days, and off oxygen support completely in another two days. She amazed both the doctors and nurses.

Karen was active and could communicate her wishes quite well with her eyes and her actions. Most Trisomy-18 babies that live just lay there and do nothing but gain weight, slowly at best, and are severely mentally retarded, unable to move much or communicate. Karen was different.

On May 1 she had learned to smile. She both gave and received love. She loved to hold our fingers or our clothes so that we couldn't get away, at least not easily. She even learned to laugh, sometimes aloud and sometimes with no sound, although we could see her little belly bouncing with laughter.

After she came home, she got upper respiratory infections and bronchitis several times, getting well each time for just a few days before something else would make her sick. She had fevers almost every day or every other day, lasting from only thirty minutes to perhaps all day. Why? Her immune system was negligible, but at least operable enough to try to fight the infections.

On December 4, Karen got a higher than normal fever, 103° to 104°, and there seemed to be no explanation. Her ears were too small to see into, and she refused to open her mouth for Dr. Allen to see her throat. Her white blood count was only slightly higher than normal. Friday, December 8, we found the cause. Her left ear must have had an infection, because fluid leaked out and crusted up on her ear. We put her on antibiotics that night. Karen had no fever from early Saturday morning through Wednesday.

On Sunday, December 10, Karen's feeding tube came out of her stomach, so we took her to the emergency room and had a #14 foley catheter put in its place. The hole had closed within five or ten minutes, and Karen was smiling and even laughing at the hospital at first, until they put the new tube in and she bled and hurt. Because the new tube slid in and out too much, and I was afraid it might puncture something inside, on Wednesday, December 13, we took Karen to Houston and had a *button* inserted to replace the feeding tube. Then she would have a flat surface on her tummy when she started to crawl or scoot, rather than a tube hanging down, to get caught on things. She was already moving her legs a lot, as if trying to crawl. She merely needed to strengthen her arms before she would be able to crawl, too. Her progress there seemed to break her out of the trisomy mold again.

She could finally hold a toy for five minutes or more. Once, completely on her own, she even picked up a plastic thermometer case that was beside her on the couch, slowly moved it up to her chest, and laid it down again, grinning and obviously pleased at her accomplishment, and watching me watch her. She could also let you know if she wasn't in the mood to do something, like picking up the thermometer case again as I coaxed her to "show Daddy how big you are." When I put her hand on the case, she let me know with her eyes that she was not interested in repeating the feat. When I tried to insist, she picked it up and threw it on the floor and gave me a look that said, "There, are you satisfied?" She did have a temper and a mind of her own.

Karen was actually old enough to be teething, getting one or two bottom teeth. It was difficult to tell with her little gums, but she definitely didn't like the pain, especially in addition to all the other aches and pains. When it hurt, it would make her so mad, or occasionally sad.

Thursday, December 14, Karen started running a fever again, first 104°, and then 105° at the doctor's office. It was pneumonia again, so we had to rush her to the hospital. There they put her on a nasal cannula for oxygen. Since they couldn't get an IV into her any place, her gastrostomy allowed her to be fed and not dehydrate. They gave her the antibiotics by injection. By Friday night, she seemed much better, and they told us that we might be able to take her home soon. The nurses told me to get some sleep. I was exhausted and was ready for sleep.

Saturday, December 16, Karen's oxygen meter started making a lot of noise, waking me up at about 6:30 a.m. She had never had a bowel movement after the nurses had inserted a laxative suppository; her diaper was still open, as they had left it. She was limp; she didn't fight me when I tried to sponge her off as before to reduce her fever. I frantically called the nurse. As she was checking Karen's vital signs, Karen's heart stopped beating. The doctors never got it started that time. She died at 7:10 a.m. Why? Why now, Lord, after she had come so far? Only six more days and it would have been her first birthday. We would have been able to watch her eat her first birthday cake, with the doctor's permission, and she would have beaten the odds again. She was progressing at a much faster pace. It just didn't make sense, but death doesn't make sense. God didn't make us originally that way, not to die, but to live forever with Him. Man brought death on himself, but why a baby? Why? As Kimi asked me the same questions and wanted to know why Karen had died after we had prayed for her healing, and she and I had both prayed for her to come back to life when Karen first died, I began to realize that even Karen's death was a miracle. I told Kimi that God always answers our prayers, just not always the way that we want or think they will be answered. God did make Karen completely well and whole; He just did it in Heaven instead of here on earth where we wanted it to occur. Surprisingly enough, Kimi seemed to understand and accept that answer. Dr. Allen, who was in the room with us, just cried with the rest of us. Unfortunately, Karen couldn't overcome one of their predicted statistics: few Trisomy-18s make it to a year old. Her life of fighting and beating the odds was over.

... a time to die... a time to mourn... (Eccl. 3:2-4 NIV).

CHAPTER TWELVE

The Greatest is Love

And so faith, hope, love abide... these three, but the greatest of these is love (I Cor. 13:13 Amplified).

Many people are familiar with the *love* chapter in the Bible (I Corinthians 13), which explains God's unconditional love and how to achieve it. Karen's presence seemed to fill our lives with the same ingredients found in this chapter—faith, hope, and love.

When Karen was transferred to Hermann Hospital at only two days old, my friend, Chris, called me at the hospital and told me that she had been praying and that Jesus had told her (not audibly, of course) that He wasn't going to take Karen from us at that time. I felt I could trust what Chris said, and I needed that word of encouragement from God right then. There was **hope**! (Hope is that word from someone that sparks the faith God put inside you, to encourage it to start growing.)

Our **faith** that God was taking care of Karen developed as we read through the Scriptures. Friends shared with us their favorite ones, Scriptures on healing for Karen and about encouragement for us. I kept them all and eventually compiled them into spiral booklets. Later I shared these booklets with other parents whose children were also in intensive care, both in Houston and in Corpus Christi. The booklets of God's Word became as much a blessing to me as they were to others. (Faith is a gift from God, for us to develop. It is being sure of what we hope for and certain of what we do not see [Heb 11:1].)

After Karen's death, some people were afraid that the faith of those who had prayed for Karen would be hindered. It shouldn't have been. People with true faith, not just the kind boasted about, know that God sometimes answers, "Yes," sometimes, "Wait," and sometimes, "No." Because He sees the whole picture and not just part of it like we do, He knows the best answer. He is always right.

The *love chapter* in the Bible says that faith and hope are important, but that the most important thing is love. Our first opportunity to demonstrate love was when I realized I was pregnant. Because of my age, the obstetrician had suggested amniocentesis, but what would have been the point? Would we have done away with the baby if it were not perfect? Of course not! We couldn't destroy what God had given us as a gift. *Behold, children are a gift of the Lord; the fruit of the womb is a reward* (Ps. 127:3 NASB).

We began to understand love in deeper, more meaningful ways as we were around Karen. Karen was not a typical baby you could show off to everyone, and simply feed her, change her, and put her to bed. No baby is truly that simple to take care of, but Karen was different. Within a few days after she was born, we found out that she **wasn't** *normal*, but she wasn't *abnormal* according to *normal* standards either. She just didn't fit the pattern for babies with her genetic disorder. Because she couldn't drink from a bottle without great effort and without the possibility of getting the food into her lungs, at five weeks we had the choice of learning to feed her through tubes or taking her home to feed her what she could eat and to watch her slowly die. With great difficulty and much anguish, we learned how to use the tubes. At six months we had to decide whether to find a doctor willing to perform necessary heart surgery on a child whose condition was considered *lethal* according to *experts* or to take her home and "enjoy her while we could." Doctors even said that if she survived surgery, she would probably be on oxygen the rest of her life. We found a caring team of cardiologists and surgeons in Corpus Christi, and Karen not only made it through surgery, but also was off of oxygen within a few days. She had a tremendous will to live and an ability to influence people's lives with her personality, her temperament, her determination, and her special kind of love. According to statistics, she should have been only a taker when it came to love and caring, but she gave to all who met her, not in an ordinary sense, but in a special way.

She loved her family and wanted and tried to be more like the rest of them, instead of being locked up in a body that wouldn't do what she wanted it to. Her drive and determination sparked the same in her family. She wasn't ready to give up and die, so we weren't ready to give up on her either; as long as she was fighting for her life, we would fight. Handicaps don't always have to be a handicap; it's a matter of perspective. Like Bruce Carroll's song says, "Sometimes miracles hide, and God will wrap some blessings in disguise."

Each child is unique and should be loved and accepted for her accomplishments within her own capabilities, rather than compared to others to determine how much love and acceptance we should give her. At the hospitals and other places we took Karen people seemed to sense our love and the importance of human life. Jesus spoke often of love in the Bible. He told His disciples that they should be different; they could be identified by their love for one another. Then He also told them that to be different, they should even love their enemies, for most anyone could love their family and closest friends. Sometimes that was very difficult, especially if it seemed like *the enemy* was *hurting* my child.

Jesus also frequently showed compassion, closely related to love, both for the crowds and for certain individuals. One group of doctors in Houston seemed to me to have compassion of a sort for the many, but not for the individual. They explained that if they performed the surgery on Karen, "the surgeon would be like an executioner," and that they shouldn't waste their time with a baby who would die anyway, but should spend their time on others who had a chance for survival. The doctors and nurses in Corpus felt that there must be a chance for Karen, even if a slim one, because we were so determined, and Karen seemed to be too. Karen was different, special, an individual, and should have been looked at that way. She wasn't just one of a group that fit into the category of Trisomy-18 babies. God made each baby, each child, each adolescent, and each adult a unique person, and we should all be seen and treated that way.

What Is Love

What is love?
Is it the time you spend with someone you care for?
Is it a look, a touch, a desire?
Is it the way your head swells and your heart beats
faster when you see that special person or even think
about that person?
Is it that proud feeling you get when that person is close?
Is it watching that person enjoy herself (or himself) and
being content?
Is it wanting to hold that person close and to cuddle a while?
Is it wanting to do whatever you can to please that person?
Is it enjoying sitting quietly beside that person and not doing
anything but being in her (or his) presence?
Is it the love for a spouse, a child, a parent, a boyfriend
or girlfriend?

Yes, it is these and more.
One song says, "Love is not a feeling; it's an act of the will."
But I think it's both.

In the end, Karen did finally have to give in. She lost her life here on earth, but her love stayed here in the hearts of all who knew her. Karen's love for others and their almost instant love for her will live on for a long time.

God showed us repeatedly by miracles and by His Word that He was taking care of Karen. He even gave me a dream in June that Karen died and came back to life, as I obeyed and did what the Word said. Like Jairus' daughter, Karen was completely healed in the dream. On the morning her heart stopped at Hermann Hospital, I thought of the dream immediately, and said, "Okay, Lord, if that's what I have to do, I will." I felt that God Himself caused her heart to start. My willingness was enough, perhaps like Abraham with Isaac, except my act of obedience was to raise her from the dead in the dream (and be scoffed at), while Abraham's was to kill Isaac.

Saturday, December 16, when her heart stopped, I thought of the dream again. Was this my real test? They told me they couldn't revive her; she was indeed dead! I asked for them to bring her to me. I held her and prayed for her to come back to life. (Kimi also prayed for her to come back to life, on the way over to the hospital.) I felt resistance. (A few weeks later, I was talking to Terri Willis about this and she mentioned that Karen did have a free will. As I napped later that afternoon, I could visualize her up in Heaven, tugging on Jesus' robe and saying, "Please don't make me go back, Jesus; please, don't make me go back.") Although I didn't understand it at the time, I remember looking at Karen's face as I held her limp body and finally saying, "Okay, Karen, I don't blame you. If I were where you are now, I wouldn't want to come back either." I quit **praying** for her to come back to life—for me—to see her become completely well someday, as God had promised. I knew I had to let her stay where she was, completely well then—no more pain, no more fevers, no more frustrations because she couldn't move around and do what her sisters could do. She could do all they could then and more. I don't know why her heart had to stop and why she had to die so soon. I do know that I had to let her go, to let her stay. I loved her that much.

There is something else I don't understand now, but will someday, I hope. After our family got home from the hospital and my husband and I were getting ready to go to the funeral home to make funeral arrangements, I was taking my shower. I was still asking myself numerous "Why?" questions, when I felt in my heart that I heard Karen tell me, "Mommy, I had to die, so you could live." Stunned, I wondered what it meant. (It did make it easier later when I had to separate and eventually divorce, because I had to go to work and wouldn't have been able to take care of her around the clock.) I don't understand yet what it really means, but I do know one thing—she loved me that much too!

CHAPTER THIRTEEN

A Mother's Reflection

As I began to deal with the reality of Karen's death, I began to see God's hand in many of the things I did. On January 11, 1990, I was reading from Mrs. Charles Cowman's devotional book, *Streams in the Desert*. The January 10 selection was an anonymous poem:

> *Is there some problem in your life to solve,*
> *Some passage seeming full of mystery?*
> *God knows, who brings the hidden things to light.*
> *He keeps the key.*
>
> *Is there some door closed by the Father's hand*
> *Which widely opened you had hoped to see?*
> *Trust God and wait—for when he shuts the door*
> *He keeps the key.*
>
> *Is there some earnest prayer unanswered yet,*
> *Or answered NOT as you had thought 'twould be?*
> *God will make clear his purpose by and by.*
> *He keeps the key.*

Have patience with your God, your patient God,
All wise all knowing no long tarrier He,
And of the door of all thy future life
He keeps the key.

Unfailing comfort, sweet and blessed rest,
To know of EVERY door he keeps the key.
That He at last when just HE sees 'tis best,
Will give it THEE.

The devotional for January 11 is even more to the point. It says, "God does not comfort us to make us comfortable, but to make us comforters."

It explains that the world is full of comfortless hearts, and, to prepare for a ministry of comforting, we must pass through the same afflictions. The special sorrows that we are passing through will some day, maybe in ten years or maybe tomorrow, allow us to tell other sufferers how we were comforted. Our experiences can help others. We can turn sorrow to comfort.[14]

Such thoughts had already occurred to me, but I wondered **what** I needed to tell others, and which others? What was I to write about Karen's life and death? Was I to try to help parents or children learn how to love and deal with a child with special problems, with death ever lurking over their heads, but with Jesus and life ever in front of them? Should I tell how never to lose faith in God, in spite of drawbacks? I knew that God would tell me what to do and when, in His time.

GOD'S PRESENCE.

On Sunday, January 21 (Stephanie's birthday), Pastor Haynes talked briefly about praise and worship and devoted most of the service to actual praise and worship. As I closed my eyes for worship, I felt I was in the presence of God, and immediately I sensed Karen's presence. She was full of joy. Now she was singing and dancing as she had so often watched Kimi do and had wanted and tried so hard to get up off the bed and do also. I was so happy for her, but I had to open my eyes. It was too much for me. I cried most of the rest of the service. (When Stephanie's Grandma Jo died, twice at our church service I felt her presence in the presence of God, and once I was sure I heard her singing. Her voice was distinct.)

Later in the worship service, I thought I heard angels singing. Their voices were so high, but it was so beautiful and so perfect. Then I thought it must have just been the ladies singing harmony when the men sang the melody in one of the songs. Later, Claire told me that she had told Suzanne Landry that she thought she had heard the angels singing and Suzanne said she had heard them before, too.

I wonder if when people die, their first assignment is to spend time in the presence of God to take in all His love and joy that they can. Then they can go out and minister to others in Heaven.

A Delicate Flower.

This afternoon (February 11, 1990) as I was cutting back the rose bushes and weeding around them, a curious thought came to me. I felt so badly about the condition that many of our plants, bushes, and trees were in, but I knew that I had been unable to take care of them properly this past year for a very good reason. I had been entrusted with a very delicate flower that required a lot of work, a lot of nurturing and special feeding, and round the clock care. Its temperature had to be regulated frequently, and it needed many other nutrients to regulate its very source of life.

Unfortunately, this delicate flower was meant to last just less than a year, and now it's time for me to take care of another garden somewhere else.

I wonder how many of us, when the weather is beautiful, and we head outside to take care of the various plants in our yards, have really asked the Head Gardener if that is where he really wants us to work today? Is there perhaps another special flower that needs tending somewhere? Or perhaps what looks like only weeds somewhere may be hiding a sturdy plant that needs only a little light to enlighten it, so that it can blossom and grow to be healthy and strong, the way it was meant to be. Perhaps there is a vine, a bush, or a tree that needs to be pruned so that it can bear good fruit.

As the weather gets nicer, and we all want to go outside and work in our yards and play in our yards, perhaps we should ask first, "Is this the garden or plant I should be tending today?"

KIMI AND GOD.

Later that day, Kimi and I experienced and had the opportunity to talk about being where God wants you to be when He needs you there.

We dropped Stephanie off at a party at 2:00 p.m. and had two errands to run—going to the post office to mail some letters and thank-you's and taking a vase of flowers to put on Karen's grave. (The post office was closer to the party, so should have been first.) I told Kimi the two things we needed to do, and she wanted to take the flowers first. We decided to stop first along the way and ask at Old America Store if they had any vases or anchors for vases that could be used at the cemetery. They didn't, so we went to Karen's grave. Kimi asked about the Taylor headstone and about Boo (her deceased grandmother's nickname) and her marker. She just wanted to stay there awhile to play and talk about Boo and Karen. I told her that we would need to leave soon, but she wasn't ready to leave. Finally, I started to cry as I read Karen's marker and began to think about her. I told Kimi that we needed to go. I remembered that we needed to go to the grocery store, too, and asked Kimi which one she would like to go to today, since it didn't really matter. As I waited for Kimi and started to get into the car, one of the elderly ladies who had been in her car on the cemetery drive around the corner from us came toward us and said that their car had stalled and asked if we would be able to help them.

I told Kimi that now I knew why we had stayed there so long today. We drove over and helped them jump-start their car. I had jumper cables and lots of experience with that problem. The ladies introduced themselves and asked what they owed us. I told them just to help whomever they could next and told them that others had already helped me with my cars many times, so I try to help whenever I can in return for past kindnesses. The older lady told me the name of her church and said that we should visit sometime. Then they both assured me that they already help others whenever they can.

It was not only a beautiful day, but a great day as well for Kimi and me!

HOLDING.

March 1, 1990:

Dear God, it hurts so much not having anyone to hold anymore, except Kimi and Stephanie, and they're not really at the holding stage any more.

My baby, whom I used to hold so much when I first brought her home from the hospital, is no longer here. She's with you now. She's really your baby anyway, but I got to love and mother her for a short time. I used to love to rock her when they brought her back to the hospital here too, after her five-day stay at Hermann Hospital, when she was two to seven days old. I would rock her and look at her, or try to feed her, for as long as I thought everyone else could stand it; the rest of my family or my friends who would bring me would watch through the window of the special care nursery or, getting tired of that, go into the waiting room and watch TV. Occasionally, someone would keep Kimi and drop me off for a while or for as long as I needed. That was great, because then I could concentrate just on her. (I still did not drive myself because of my C-section delivery.)

As Karen grew, she didn't always like to be held as long, but she liked to have us right close by. She liked to sit in her car seat, or lie on the pillow on my bed or one of the girls' beds, or lie on the couch beside us. But she still desired to be rocked enough to satisfy that need in me. Then, just as I was working with her to help her move on to the next stage, moving about for herself, suddenly and unexpectedly she was gone....

It's so hard now, because we hadn't quite moved into that next stage together. She can move about by herself where she is now, but I'm still here, still trying to move forward....

MY CHILDREN.

Recently, it has been brought to my attention that Stephanie is no longer a little or big girl, but is becoming a young lady, and a beautiful one at that. I've noticed it, but sometimes it helps to have it brought to my attention again.

Yesterday, I realized something about Kimi too. Because of the whole-hearted way she loves the Lord and the boldness she has in singing about it and praying for others, I feel that there is a special call on her life. My job is to protect her from whatever or whoever might try to stifle or quench that love or boldness. Her little spirit, soul, and body need to be protected. I thought about how Moses' mother must have felt when she just knew he was special and didn't let Pharaoh's men or orders destroy him, but saved him as long she could and then trusted him to God for the rest.

After those thoughts, imagine my shock when Kimi showed me her projects from children's church last night—some bulrushes and a baby Moses in the basket picture!

I began to realize something different about Karen, too. During the worship part of the service, Pastor Haynes had talked about entering into the throne room of God, into His very presence. It made me think about another time when I had entered into worship and sensed Karen's presence as I felt God's presence. It had hurt the time before, but I chanced it again. I needed God's presence to touch me and heal some hurts. As before, I sensed Karen's presence too, and this time I could almost see her far off near a large tree, though not clearly. I wasn't sure if she was sitting or standing. This time, however, I realized something different about her. For over a year I had been praying for her. Now she was praying for me.

NOT IN VAIN!

During Karen's funeral service John, our pastor, had mentioned that Karen's life was not in vain, because in less than a year she had touched more lives than most of us do in a whole lifetime. She was a fighter, and had the personality and temperament to go along with it. However, her ability to touch lives didn't end with her death. At the funeral service, the things God led John to say had an impact on a lot of people, not only those from our church, but family, doctors, nurses, friends in the SAR and DAR, and who knows how many others. Many were in tears. People commented to John, my husband, and myself about it. It had had a positive effect. Eyes were opened or at least opened wider.

Her outreach didn't end with her funeral either. Several friends have donated Gideon Bibles in her name. Only God knows how many will be touched by those.

The way we live our lives and our continued faith and trust in God, in spite of her death, are other ways that neither her life nor her death were or will be in vain. What the devil meant for harm, since he comes to steal, kill, and destroy (John 10:10), God will use for good and to His glory. I don't know how just now, but He will, because His Word says He will (Romans 8:28).

LOSING A CHILD, A JOB.

Losing a child for a mother is similar to a man being early retired or fired from his job—from a job that he really liked, or loved.

A mother knows that some day she must lose or let go of a child as she goes off to college or gets married, but she gets to work up to that gradually, letting go a little bit at a time as the child matures. A man losing his job early is not prepared either. He knows that he will retire some day and probably looks forward to having time to himself for things he likes to do, but not suddenly or too soon. He's just not ready. A mother looks forward to the freedom when the children will be grown and she can pursue her own interests or hobbies. However, if a mother loses a child by death, especially a child who has been a 24-hour-a-day job, a child who was chronically ill, she has her job, a large part of her life, and her love all snatched away from her at once; it is almost too much to bear. It is like part of her has been ripped off. The only way for her to bear it is through Jesus, for he alone can mend all tears.

A DREAM.

One night (April 1990) I had an unusual dream. I was at the passenger side of my car standing on the outside with the door open. Karen's car seat was in the front seat facing forward (which it never was) and she was in it. As I realized that it was Karen, she turned and smiled at me, as thought she was so happy to see me. Then I woke up, but I went back to sleep as quickly as I could.

TIME.

Today we are so used to the convenience of microwaves, fast foods, and all kinds of gadgets that do work for us faster, that we often forget that some things still do best only with time.

We often say a prayer, and then expect an answer in whatever time span we imagine as reasonable. Probably many times we think that God has said, "No," when He has simply said, "Yes, but in My time and My way, not yours." Since His vision is eternal, rather than limited to time as we know it, He can always do what is best for us, whether we realize and believe it or not. We just need to allow Him that privilege.

Often, when we pray for healing, we want a miracle right now. Sometimes we get it, but often we have to wait for the slow, steady process of healing. In that process, we usually develop more faith, trust, and love for out Heavenly Father. When we walk with our daddies, rather than run, we develop a better relationship with them as we communicate; the same is true with our Heavenly Daddy. Sometimes the process is easy, although tedious; sometimes it involves hurt or pain; but the end result is still healing.

In December 1989, we lost a very special daughter who had fought for her life for almost a year. We fought with her all the way. Since she wasn't expected to live for even a month because of her chromosome problem, we saw many healings in her life as she progressed. Although we had hoped that she would be healed here on earth and live a long, full life, we know that where she is now, she is completely healed. Her healing process is complete, and ours has just begun. Grief is a long process too, just like any other healing can be. In March, I wrote about how I miss holding Karen, and how that must be worked through too, in time.

BLESSINGS.

If we keep praising God for His blessings, He keeps pouring out His blessings on us; but we don't always recognize them right away, for sometimes they seem disguised as something else (July 21, 1991).

LAUGHTER—THE BEST MEDICINE!

God has to have a sense of humor, or He wouldn't have given us one, especially for use when we need to reduce tension or stress, to lighten up when things seem to weigh down on us. Many times when I was struggling with the weight of Karen's illness or the problems in my marriage, I would awaken with a joke or funny picture of something in my mind, to lift the burdens and lighten up my day. Thank God for humor and laughter. What a blessing!

HUGS AND TEARS HEAL AND RESTORE.

Last December (1990), in the week covering Karen's birthday on December 16 and the first anniversary of her death on December 22, I took a week off from work so that Stephanie, Kimi, and I could go visit old friends. I had been dreading the anniversary of Karen's death, not knowing how I would act, or react. I needed to refresh and revive my mind, body, and spirit. I needed those much-needed hugs from the people who were important in my life, who were my close friends, who understood, or who at least cared, even if they didn't really understand. At the end of the week, when it was time to return, my spirit was soaring again. I was exhilarated! A little more of the pain had been squeezed out, drop-by-drop, with hugs and with the tears. (July 25, 1991)

THE GREATEST SURGEON

As I read an article in the July 1991 Reader's Digest entitled, "The Boy Who Surprised Everyone," about Ian Hudson, who was 6 years old and severely disabled physically by cerebral palsy, but who excelled mentally and emotionally in a gifted and talented class for kindergarten through second graders, I couldn't help but think of Karen. It hurts that I don't still have her here with me to enjoy her tiniest accomplishments, which were always the result of a lot of effort on her part. Like Ian, she didn't let her physical disabilities stop her or keep her from trying. Her determination and her love and something special about her were obvious to all. Actually, sometimes her stubbornness and her temper were more obvious than her love, but her special love was there. I remember different people telling Pat and me that we needed to stick together and avoid strife at all costs to stand against the devil and sickness for Karen's sake. We needed to stand together as a couple to pray and believe for her health and her life. I remember trying very hard to do this, and becoming more and more like a non-person, trying more and more to love (or *walk in love*) and avoid strife, and giving in more and more to controlling demands, trying to avoid confrontation and the release of an outpouring of unjust accusations and a grown up display of a temper tantrum. Somehow, I couldn't believe that that was what God really wanted. *At all costs* must have limits. Even Karen seemed sense the dissension. (Although her health responded quickly and positively to prayer, it also frequently responded negatively to strife in the home.) *At all costs* shouldn't include dying to self and giving that self totally to another person rather than to God. It also doesn't include making one child's physical health more important than another's emotional health. (I realized that on Thanksgiving 1989.) Each child is equally important.

If you're dealing with a lot of stress from taking care of a chronically ill child, don't let the anger you feel over the cold or inhumane treatment by doctors or others make you act in a harmful way, or to become bitter. All your energies (what little you have at times) need to be focused on helping your baby get well and stay well. If your anger can be turned into something constructive, great! If not, try to diffuse it as best you can.

If we waste time trying to get even with doctors or anyone else, *just to show them* and not to actually deal with a situation affecting our child at the time or in the near future, it only hurts us. We need to be positive in order to help other parents around us who are hurting more than we are or don't know what to do. Our babies need us to be positive, too, to fill the room with love and caring, not anger or hate or bitterness.

Sometimes I wonder if Karen's heart was the only one touched by that knife in Corpus Christi. Was there surgery being performed there on *our* hearts then, or later because of that surgery, to remove some of the things that destroy our lives, things that choke us until we can hardly breathe, like hatred, bitterness, envy, anger, and their close cousins? A lot of those were removed from our hearts gradually, by the Greatest Surgeon in the world.

CHAPTER FOURTEEN

What Siblings Say

aren's impact on people's lives didn't end when the funeral did. It didn't end when her mother put to paper all her thoughts, memories, and feelings about her very special child. No, Karen's gift of love lives on in her siblings and in others who knew her. This chapter is a compilation of a picture, which communicates as much or more than words, and a poem and stories written about Karen by her sisters, who each dealt with her life, her illness, and her death in different ways and at different times.

I begin with a picture her four-year-old sister, Kimi, gave me for Karen after she visited her baby sister in the hospital.

This is how Kimi saw her baby sister in the hospital, in a crib with rails on the sides and attached by wires to an oxygen monitor and an IV. Notice the usual hospital gown and the arms out to the side. Karen's arms were usually safety-pinned to the sheets to keep her from pulling out the needle and tube to the IV, and the tube to the ventilator, which was usually down her throat. I thought Kimi was very perceptive for a four-year-old. It was drawn on a paper towel.

Kimi also thought that she felt Karen's influence shortly after Karen's death. After the funeral was behind us, Kimi started in on Christmas. She wanted a white Christmas, with snow, like it should be. We tried to explain that it hardly ever snows in Lake Jackson or other areas near Houston in December, especially at Christmas time. When that explanation wasn't enough, we told her to pray about it, since it was so important to her. Imagine our surprise when we woke up on December 22, only to find snow on the ground! We all agreed that Karen must have had some *pull* up there, at least for that day, her birthday. What a wonderful gift for Karen's birthday!

Kimi and I talked and cried about Karen frequently after her death. Kimi was five then. However, it was more difficult for Stephanie, then in fifth grade, to talk about Karen much. I didn't get a real glimpse of her thoughts about Karen until she began to write about her in middle school. All individuals, both adults and children, have their own way of grieving, and we need to respect that individuality, even if we don't understand it. On September, 10, 1990, for a reading class in sixth grade, Steph wrote:

My Most Memorable Experience

My most memorable experience was my baby sister, Karen. It all started in December 1988 when she was born. Karen was born with Trisomy 18. The doctors said that she would probably not live to be a month, but they were wrong.

When she was born, she had bad heart problems and didn't gain weight easily, so she had to stay in the hospital until she was five weeks old. Then when she was about five and a half months old, she had to be life-flighted to Hermann Hospital. She stayed there for a month. While she was there, they determined that she needed surgery on her heart. The cardiologists at Texas Children's Hospital would not work on Karen's heart, because they said that she had too many other problems and probably would not live through the surgery. We finally took her to Corpus Christi after a month at Hermann. The cardiologist there did operate on her, and she did fine. She was there about two weeks. She was in and out of hospitals most of her life.

When she was born, she also had problems sucking and swallowing, so my mom would have to put tubes down her nose or mouth and through her throat to her stomach to feed her. When she was at Hermann, they put a tube directly into her stomach. It was called a G-tube (gastrostomy tube).

Karen died six days before her first birthday, which was December 22. She got pneumonia, and it caused heart failure and respiratory failure. Karen was a whole lot of fun. I really miss her. I wish that I could have known her better and longer than I did.

Two weeks later, on September 24, 1990, she wrote for a language-arts class:

The Pain

It was December 22, 1988 at 3:49 p.m. when Karen Elizabeth was born. She was born with Trisomy 18, which is an incurable disease. This was a hard time for me. I could not go to very many people's houses, because my mom could not take Karen out of the house. Karen had to go to Corpus

Christi that summer to get banding on her pulmonary artery, so I had to stay with my cousins. I stayed there for several weeks. She lived to be 11 months, three weeks, and one day old. She died on December 16, 1989 at 7:10 a.m., while in the hospital from pneumonia. When she died, it was very hard for me; she was a part of my life. I went to counselors and a counselor at school to try to help me cope with her death. They helped me a whole lot. I do not have as much grief now.

I will miss Karen. She was fun to have around, though she was in and out of hospitals most of her life.

In May 1994, she wrote again about Karen for an English class, rewriting a paper from eighth grade:

A Year of Hope

My most memorable moment was one of joy, fear, and tears. It began a little over five years ago, on December 22, 1988.

1988 began as a good year. I kept busy with school and after-school activities, such as dancing. Near the middle of the year it began to get better; my mother told us she was pregnant. Everyone was happy and couldn't wait to have a baby around the house again. My little sister was now about four; too old to be treated like a baby. Because my mother was over thirty-five, the doctor suggested that my mom have amniocentesis done to check the baby's health. My mom decided not to have it done because if something had been wrong, she would not have aborted it anyway. In the last month of her pregnancy, we found out that if nothing were done, the baby would come out breech. This could injure it. Mom had to go to the doctor and have the baby turned. Later she had to have a C-section to remove the baby because other problems occurred.

Once out, Karen Elizabeth Taylor was a pretty, healthy looking baby, though under weight, weighing only 3 lbs. 13 oz. Because of her size, she had to be kept in an incubator the first few days. After a couple of days she got pneumonia and had to be taken by ambulance to Hermann Hospital in Houston, Texas. Once at Hermann, the doctors found out that she had Trisomy 18, a disease in which the baby has an extra #18 chromosome. They also discovered that because of the disease, her mouth was not formed properly, so that she could not suck well on a bottle. After five days at Hermann, she was returned to the hospital in Lake Jackson. There the doctors told my mother that she could either learn to tube feed Karen—stick a tube down her mouth/nose to her stomach—or take her home and try to feed her and watch her slowly die. My mom chose to learn to tube feed her. After going from hospital to hospital, Karen was finally allowed to go home.

It was fun having her around, but I didn't get to go many places because my mom could not take the chance on getting her ill. When Karen was five and a half months, she had to go back to the hospital because she had pneumonia again. This time they life-flighted her to Hermann Hospital. There they found a tiny hole in Karen's heart. The doctors at the Texas Children's Center in Houston would not operate; they believed that the Trisomy 18 made her chance of living pretty slim. We finally found a doctor in Corpus Christi that agreed to do the operation. Karen was flown from Houston to the Children's Hospital in Corpus Christi. Once the operation was completed, she was allowed to go home again.

I loved having Karen around. She looked so cute sitting in her rocker [car seat] and watching Kimi, my other sister, and me dance and jump around. You could just tell from the expression on Karen's face that she wanted to be up and jumping. Although she couldn't get up, Karen never just sat in her chair. She always had her leg propped up, and smiled at every-

thing. Karen seemed to spend most of her life in the hospital. I remember once when my step-dad took my sister and me to see Karen at Hermann. It scared us at first because she was hooked up to many machines. Karen also had little needle pricks in her foot. They had to put the IV in her foot instead of her arm, because she kept pulling it out of her arm. While Karen was in the hospital, the doctors asked my mom why she wanted to have heart surgery for Karen. They feared that after the surgery Karen probably would have to be on a respirator the rest of her life. My mom told them as long as Karen was fighting, she was fighting. This is one thing that I admired in Karen—even as a baby she knew something was going on and never gave up hope. In June of 1989, the doctors put a G-tube (gastrostomy tube) in Karen's stomach to feed her, because she kept pulling the tubes out of her nose and mouth. This way she could not pull it out.

About six months later, on December 14, Karen had to go back to the hospital for pneumonia. She started to get better, and they took her off the oxygen machine on December 15. The doctors told my mom that Karen probably could go home in the next few days. At 7:00 a.m. on December 16, my mom woke up; the machine to measure the oxygen level in Karen's blood was beeping loudly. Mom checked Karen and wiped her forehead to make the fever go down. Karen didn't fight back as usual; she was limp. Mom got the nurse to come in, and the nurse checked Karen's pulse and other vital signs. Just as the nurse was saying that the vital signs weren't good, but weren't bad either, Karen jolted and her heart stopped. The nurses and doctors all rushed in with various equipment and mom had to leave the room. They tried to save Karen, but couldn't. Even for a baby, Karen touched many peoples' lives. She taught us never to give up when we think there is hope.

After Kimi entered school and matured, she too wrote about Karen for class assignments. In third grade, she wrote a cinquain poem (five lines):

Karen

Karen
Crying, caring
Wiggling, smiling, laughing
Happy little baby girl
Baby

Later, in October 1996, in sixth grade, Kimi wrote:

Family, Friends, and a Funeral

Although Karen only lived for almost a year, she touched many people's lives. Karen was my baby sister, my only **whole** *sister, and I don't mean whole as in in one piece, but I mean it as the same mom* **and** *dad. When I was only four, she was born on December 22, 1988. Yes, she was a very different child, but different in a very special way. She had Trisomy 18, which means that she had three instead of two of the eighteenth chromosome. (You get one chromosome from your mom and one from your dad in each of 23 sets. Each chromosome contains many pairs of genes.) Trisomy 18 caused many problems, including retardation and swallowing difficulties. We had to feed Karen through a tube. At first, my parents had to insert the tube through her nose or mouth and into her stomach, but she would always pull it out. When she was big enough for surgery at six months, the doctors sewed a gastrostomy tube directly into her stomach through the skin near her belly button. It was an ugly yellowy tan color, rubbery, and shaped like a T with a tube coming out of the stem. My parents would put the formula into this thing that looked kind of* *like a plastic syringe used to give shots, only longer, wider, and without a needle. Then they would put the end of the syringe into the tube and slowly push the formula in. Sounds fun, huh? Once Mom and I were sitting and talking on my bed near Karen. I reached over and put my arm around my baby sister. Though I barely touched her on the stomach, the tube popped out. The food in her stomach started squirting out and looked gross. I was afraid I had "hurt my baby sissy," and started crying and saying I was so sorry. We put towels over the hole to stop it up, and it closed within a few minutes. Then we rushed Karen to the emergency room and the doctor there had to put a temporary catheter tube into her stomach. Several weeks later Mom was afraid that the new tube might puncture Karen's stomach, because it slid in and out of the hole, although not completely. Since Karen was beginning to try to crawl, Mom was also afraid that the tube might get pulled out and decided to allow the doctors to put a button in place of the tube. It looked like a flat donut with a very small hole and a cover attached to plug up the hole. When it was plugged, it looked similar to the part of a stethoscope that you put up against your heart. The button would lay flat against her skin, unless she was being fed.*

*Karen also had a serious heart defect, caused by Trisomy 18. I will try to make this simple, but it is pretty complicated. Your heart has four chambers and they hold blood with different amounts of oxygen in them. [She drew a picture to accompany her paper to help the reader understand.] Her heart had a hole between the four chambers, more toward the bottom. The blood that just came **from** the **lungs**, or the 100% oxygenated blood, would mix with the old blood coming from the body and going **to** the **lungs**. She would end up having **not** 100% oxygenated blood going to her body and* *brain. Her brain would say, "Help! I need more oxygen. Pump faster and get me oxygen from the lungs." Her heart and lungs would get so overworked that her lungs would get too much blood to handle. This congestion made it difficult to breathe and would often lead to pneumonia, an inflammation of the lungs caused by some type of infection.*

*Though she didn't live a full life span, she sure showed the doctors. They didn't think she'd live one month, but she lived almost twelve months. Trisomy-18 babies usually don't have muscle tone, but she developed it at about three weeks (after much prayer). Especially when nurses at the hospital **knew** that her IVs and ventilator tubes were secure, Karen usually succeeded in kicking and squirming until the tubes and things came off. She didn't want to be **chained down** for the rest of her life; she wanted to get up and play.*

*Doing things **her way** was normal for Karen at home and in the hospital. Until she was about eleven months old, she couldn't hold things like most babies, much less pick things up on her own. One day, she got my mom really excited as she watched Mom watch her pick up a plastic baby thermometer case which was lying on the couch beside the baby seat she was sitting in. She slowly and carefully moved it to her stomach then up to her chest and gave Mom a big triumphant grin. Mom went berserk and ran to tell Dad and had him come to watch. Dad and Mom urged Karen to do it again, but she stubbornly refused. Finally, Karen raised the thermometer case once again, pulled it up to her stomach, and then almost defiantly threw the case on the floor. Mom burst out laughing; Dad wasn't sure what to think. It would have been funny to watch a little baby act so independent.*

Determination was one thing Karen did not lack. She was a born fighter and fought until her death. Although she fought, she loved unconditionally as an innocent child, and Mom and I would call her "our little angel."

I used to dance around and sing and Karen would watch me, her eyes moving with my motions. You could see by the way she watched, that she wanted so, so much to be able to get up and dance, move around, and walk.

*You know how a lot of babies do not like to be **bothered** by little kids; well, with Karen and me it was different. Sometimes, when my mom, dad, or older sister would hold her and she would not stop crying, they would give her to me to hold and she would stop. We had a very special bond.*

*Karen also showed that God has a sense of humor. Once, when some **brain** doctors came to examine her **brain**, for some reason they opened her **diaper** (which seemed odd). At that moment Karen had a big, gross b.m. (messy diaper). Mom had realized earlier that Karen was wet and suggested that she might need to change her diaper, but of course, she did not realize that Karen had had a b.m. As the doctors put their noses higher in the air, they said, "Plleeease do!" When my mom realized what Karen had done, she almost cracked up laughing out loud, for she laughed and laughed inside.*

*A lot of Karen's life was spent in hospitals. At two days old she was rushed to a Houston hospital because of aspiration pneumonia, and was sent back to Lake Jackson's hospital where she stayed until she was five weeks old and not quite five pounds yet. When she was almost six months old, she was life-flighted to Houston again for pneumonia and stayed there for a month until she was flown to Corpus Christi for heart surgery. The surgeon put a **band** on the artery going from the heart to the lungs to slow down the blood flow. He had to break her ribs to get to her heart. It was risky surgery, but her chances without it were zero. Luckily, she did not go through all that pain for nothing.*

It was not a shock when Karen got pneumonia and went to the hospital the last time, for she got it and fevers frequently. After that time she never had it again; she never had to go to the hospital again either. On Thursday, December 14, 1989, her fever went up to 104°F. (100° to 102° was normal for her.) Our doctor put her in the hospital with pneumonia again. That night her fever went up to 106° and 107°, but by Friday evening she looked like she was doing better, and we thought we would get to take her home soon. Our hopes were high! On Saturday morning, December 16, her oxygen monitor started beeping to show that her oxygen level was very low. The noise woke up Mom, who had finally fallen asleep. She rushed to Karen, who was not moving. As she wiped her head with the cloth to bring her fever down as she had so often done, this time Karen didn't fight her by kicking or squirming. Frantically, Mom called the nurse, who took Karen's vital signs (pulse, temperature, etc.). Just as the nurse told my mom that her vital signs weren't bad, although not good either, Karen suddenly jolted and my mom knew that her heart had stopped and that she had died. Mom felt totally helpless and empty. She called us at home, and we all came to the hospital and cried together until there were no tears left, or so we thought. We still cry sometimes now, though seven years later.

*For the funeral, my mom wanted to put Karen's new **First Christmas** doll in Karen's casket. I really wanted that doll! I was thinking, "Mom should let me have the dolly so that it won't go to waste." Of course, my mom didn't agree, and, being only five, I thought, "She is acting really stupid. Doesn't she know anything?" Finally I blurted out, "Don't you know it's just gonna rot!?!" It made her cry more, but she also looked a little like she was laughing inside. She said, "No!" but I got over it.*

Though I miss Karen very much and still feel like crying

sometimes, I know that she is better off where she is. No more pneumonia, no more pain! Our little angel is home.

In October 1998, in eighth grade, Kimi upgraded her report for language class, but kept the same name. The words are similar, but it's more mature:

Family, Friends, and a Funeral

*Although Karen lived for only about a year, she touched many people's lives. Karen was my baby sister, my only **whole** sister. By whole I do not mean **in one piece**, but that we have the same mom **and** dad. While I was only four, she was born on December 22, 1988. Yes, she was a different child, but different in a very special way.*

She had Trisomy 18, which means that she had three instead of two of the eighteenth chromosome. (You get one chromosome from your mom and one from your dad in each of 23 pairs. Each chromosome contains many sets of genes.) Trisomy 18 caused her many problems, including retardation, heart problems, eating difficulties, and failure to thrive.

Karen's heart defect was serious. Every heart has four chambers, which hold blood with different amounts of oxygen in them. Her heart had a hole between the two lower chambers. The blood that just came from the lungs, or the 100% oxygenated blood, would mix with the old blood coming from the body and going to the lungs. She would end up having less than 100% oxygenated blood going to her body and brain. "Help! I need more oxygen," her brain would say. "Pump faster and get me more oxygen from the lungs." Her heart and lungs would get so overworked that her lungs would get too much blood to handle. This congestion made it difficult to breathe and would often lead to pneumonia, an inflammation of the lungs caused by some type of infection.

Another thing that caused her pneumonia was getting formula in her lungs. Because the roof of her mouth was too high, and the soft palate at the back was not formed correctly, the formula often went directly into her lungs. Other times, it went into her stomach and sloshed back up and into her lungs, because the sphincter muscle at the top of her stomach did not stay closed.

We had to feed Karen through a tube to make the food go directly into her stomach and stay there. At first, my parents had to insert the tube through her nose or mouth and into her stomach, but she would often pull it out. My mom or dad would put the formula into a plastic syringe like one used to give shots, only longer, wider, and without a needle. Then they would put the end of the syringe into the tube and slowly push in the formula. Sounds fun, huh?

When Karen was big enough for surgery at six months, the doctors sewed a gastrostomy tube directly into her stomach through the skin near her belly button. It was an ugly yellowy-tan color, rubbery, and shaped like a T with a tube coming out of the stem. After this surgery, we could feed her almost continuously with a feeding pump. This allowed Mom to sleep more and not wake up every three hours to feed Karen to keep her alive.

About six months later, I was lying on my bed near Karen and talking to my mom. Reaching over, I put my arm around my baby sister. Though I barely touched her stomach, the tube popped out, causing the food in her stomach to squirt out in every direction, looking very disgusting. Afraid I had "hurt my baby sissy," I started crying and saying I was sorry. We put towels over the hole to apply pressure, and it closed within a few minutes. Next we rushed Karen to the emergency room, where the doctor put a temporary catheter tube into her stomach.

Several weeks later, Mom was afraid that the new tube might puncture Karen's stomach, because it slid in and out of the hole, although not completely. Since Karen was beginning to try to crawl, Mom was also afraid that the tube might get pulled out and decided to allow the doctors to put a **button** *in place of the tube. Similar to a flat donut, it had a small hole and a cover attached to plug up the hole. After it was plugged, it looked similar to the part of a stethoscope that you put up against your heart. The button would lie flat against her skin, unless she was being fed.*

Almost a fourth of Karen's life was spent in hospitals. At two days old she was rushed to a Houston hospital because of aspiration pneumonia, and was sent back to Lake Jackson's hospital five days later. She stayed there until she was five weeks old and not quite five pounds. When she was almost six months old, she was life-flighted to Houston again for pneumonia and stayed there for a month until she was flown to Corpus Christi for heart surgery. The surgeon put a band on the artery going from the heart to the lungs to slow down the blood flow. He had to break her ribs to get to her heart. Even though it was risky surgery, her chances without it were zero. Luckily, she did not go through all that pain for nothing.

Though she did not live a full life span, she really surprised the doctors. Statistics show that most Trisomy-18 babies do not live a month, let alone six months, but she lived almost a year. Trisomy-18 babies usually do not have muscle tone, but she developed it at about three weeks (after much prayer). Even if nurses at the hospital were sure that her IVs and ventilator tubes were secure, Karen usually succeeded in kicking and squirming until the tubes and things came out. Without her realizing it, this exercised and developed her muscles.

Karen also showed that God has a sense of humor. Once, when some neurologists (brain doctors) came to examine her **brain**, for some reason they opened her **diaper**, which seemed odd. (Since Trisomy-18 babies often have enlarged genitals, apparently their curiosity outweighed their professionalism.) At that moment Karen had a large, nauseating bowel movement. Mom had realized earlier that Karen was wet and suggested that she might need to change her diaper while it was open. Of course, she did not realize that Karen had just had a bowel movement. As the doctors put their noses higher in the air, they said, "Plleeease do!" When my mom realized what Karen had done, she almost cracked up laughing out loud, for she agreed totally with Karen's opinion of the doctors.

Doing things **her way** was normal for Karen at home and in the hospital. Until she was about eleven months old, she could not hold things more than a few seconds, like most babies, much less pick things up on her own. One day she got my mom really excited. Watching Mom watch her, she picked up a plastic thermometer case, which was lying on the couch beside the baby seat she was in. Slowly and carefully, she moved it to her stomach then up to her chest and gave Mom a big triumphant grin. Mom went berserk and ran to tell Dad and ask him to come watch. Dad and Mom urged Karen to do it again, but she stubbornly refused. Finally, Karen raised the thermometer case once again, pulled it up to her stomach, and then almost defiantly threw the case on the floor. Mom burst out laughing; Dad was not sure what to think. It would have been hysterical to watch a little baby, who was supposed to be seriously retarded, act so independently. Many babies do not like to be **bothered** and played with by little kids, but with Karen and me it was different. Sometimes, when my mom, dad, or older sister would hold her and she would not

stop crying, they would give her to me to hold and she usual-
ly would stop. We had a very special bond.

As a little girl, I used to dance around and sing, and
Karen would watch me, her eyes moving with my motions.
You could see by the way she watched, that she wanted so
much to be able to get up and dance, move around, and walk
*like her big sister. She did not want to be **chained down** for*
the rest of her life; she wanted to get up and play.

Determination was one thing Karen did not lack. Born a
fighter, she fought until her death. Although she fought, she
also loved unconditionally as an innocent child, and Mom
and I would call her "our little angel."

It was not a shock when Karen got pneumonia and went
to the hospital the last time, for she got it frequently. After that
time she never had it again; she never had to go to the hospi-
tal again either. On Thursday, December 14, her fever went
up to 105.7°F (100° to 102° was normal for her.), and our
doctor put her in the hospital. That night her fever went up
to 106° and 107°, but by Friday evening she looked as though
she were doing better. We thought we would get to take her
home soon. Our hopes were high!

On Saturday morning, December 16, 1989, her oxygen
monitor started beeping to show that her oxygen level was very
low. The noise woke up Mom, who had finally fallen asleep.
Rushing to the crib, Mom realized that Karen was not mov-
ing. As she wiped Karen's head with the cloth to bring the
fever down, as she had so often done, this time Karen did not
fight her by kicking or squirming. Frantically, Mom called the
nurse, who took Karen's vital signs (pulse, temperature, etc.).
Just as the nurse told my mom that the vital signs were not
bad, although not good either, Karen suddenly jolted and my
mom knew that her heart had stopped and that she had died.

Mom felt totally helpless and empty; the child she had loved was now ripped out of her life, leaving a hole in her once-filled heart. She called us at home, and we all came to the hospital and cried together until there were no tears left, or so we thought. We still cry occasionally, although it has been almost nine years.

Because I was only five, I did not realize the solemnity of death and funerals. Even though I was sad and missed my **baby sissy**, *I was happy for her, because she was in heaven. For the funeral, my mom wanted to put Karen's new* **First Christmas** *doll in Karen's casket. I really wanted that doll! "Mom should let me have the dolly so that it won't go to waste," I was thinking. Of course, my mom didn't agree, and being a little girl, I thought, "She is acting really stupid. Doesn't she know anything?" Finally I blurted out, "Don't you know it's just gonna rot!?!" It made her cry more, but she also looked as if she were laughing inside. Even though she cried, "No!" I got over it.*

Though I miss Karen very much and still feel like crying sometimes, I know that she is better off where she is. No more pneumonia, no more pain! Our little angel is home.

Was Karen's Life in Vain?

The birth of Karen was a great day for rejoicing! But within a matter of hours, it became obvious that things were not as they should be. The nurses began to look intently at Karen, checking for certain signs.

Karen was diagnosed with Trisomy 18 Syndrome. These babies are usually feeble and have a limited capacity for survival. They have a weak cry, poor sucking capabilities, usually have to be fed through a tube, and normally fail to thrive. Thirty per cent die within the first month and 50% by two months. Only 10% survive the first year, severely mentally impaired.

Karen was only three pounds and thirteen ounces when born and had a large hole in her heart.

Society would say that Karen was born with a handicap… and extra medical attention would be needed, not to mention extra care, love, and patience! During her short lifetime, she has been in and out of several hospitals, where wonderful doctors and nurses have fought for her life!

Karen was a fighter, beating the odds… clearly responding to prayer. Scores of people and churches have prayed for, loved, and cared for her since her birth. She has required a special mother and father, who have put the child's needs first, doing everything for her that possibly could be done. No expense was spared in the fight for her life.

Robin and Pat: I can honestly say that I speak for the entire community when I say that you are two of the most special people that we have ever known. Most of us would have crumbled under the load you have faithfully carried.

Was Karen's life in vain? She only lived a year, and never said a word! But Karen has probably touched more lives in her short life-time than many touch in a full lifetime. Robin has had the opportunity to minister to numbers of parents, witnessing and giving Scriptures of hope to each. The concern of doctors, nurses, and even chaplains has not gone unnoticed or unappreciated.

By Karen's endurance of pain and discomfort, medical tests, and all kinds of support systems, we have been inspired to greater patience and learned better how to meet life's variety of adversities, not to mention showing more compassion to others who are hurting! She has been a constant reminder of how wonderful life is and how very complex the human body is. In fact, it is a miracle any-one turns out *normal* when you consider just how many things can go wrong at birth!

In no way was this life in vain, for we can all learn from her… to appreciate our good health… and to live each day as if it were our last!

I want to read a story I came across last night, not for its doc-trinal content, of course.

A meeting was held quite far from earth.
"It's time again for another birth,"
Said the angels to the Lord above.
"This special child will need much love.

Her progress may seem very slow.
Accomplishments will not show,
And she will require extra care
From folks she meets way down there.

She may not run or laugh or play;
Her thoughts may seem quite far away.
In many ways she won't adapt,
And she'll be known as handicapped.

So let's be careful where she's sent.
We want her life to be content.
Please, Lord, find parents who
Will do a special job for you.

They will not realize right away
The leading role they're asked to play,
But with this child sent from above
Comes stronger faith and richer love;

And soon they'll know the privilege given
On caring for this gift from heaven.
Their precious charge, so meek and mild
Is heaven's very special child."

© Edna Massimilla

As believers in the Lord Jesus Christ, we can turn to Him for reassurance in our time of need… resting upon His Word, when we read the words of Paul, To be absent from the body is to be present with the Lord.

Jesus Himself said, in John 11:25-26,

I am the resurrection and the life: he that believeth in me, though he were dead, yet shall he live; and whosoever liveth and believeth in me shall never die.

Baby Karen is today in a far better place... at home with Jesus... no more tears, no more pain, sorrow, or discomfort. Friends, if you don't know this wonderful Savior Jesus Christ, let me just say, "He loves you, and He loves little children."

(Charlotte Stark sang acappela *Jesus Loves Me*.)

(The above were words by our pastor, taken from Karen's funeral.)

Appendix

Voice of the People

Reader asks important questions

TO THE FACTS:

Recently I heard reporters on the news talking about the people arrested outside of abortion clinics. Today I got literature in the mail about abortion and it made me realize that each of us really needs to ask ourselves, "How precious is a baby to me?"

Baby Karen was born in December with a genetic problem called Trisomy 18. She was small for a full-term baby, three pounds, 13 ounces, and had to stay in the hospital more than a month until she was large enough to go home.

Her condition could have been detected early in the pregnancy with amniocentesis, and her life could have been terminated. Her parents chose not to do the test.

Because her mouth was small and not shaped prop-

THE BRAZOPORT FACTS   **Sunday, March 12, 1989**

erly inside, she was unable to take enough formula by bottle without getting it in her nose, causing her to spit out the formula and give up on eating.

When it was time for her to leave the hospital, her parents had three options: Learning to feed her through a tube in her nose or mouth, having a feeding tube put into her stomach, or feeding her what she could take by bottle and watching her slowly starve to death. She is fed from a tube in her nose or mouth.

Most Trisomy 18 babies don't make it past the first month, but some make it one to three years. A few live longer. Actually, do any of us have a guarantee on the length of our children's lives? Many children each year are killed or disabled in accidents. Is a short expected life span and possible disabilities a good reason to do away with a baby?

Karen, in most ways, is like any other baby. She looks around, makes funny faces and funny noises, smiles and cries. She likes to be held, rocked, sung to, and snuggled. She is a lot of work, but she is a blessing. She could have been killed in the womb or allowed to starve to death at home, but she wasn't. How precious is a baby?

Robin Taylor
Lake Jackson

Resources

Although I didn't actually write about them, I wanted to express my gratefulness to an organization, The Compassionate Friends, which helped me tremendously after Karen's death. I attended meetings regularly at the Brasosport Chapter. The members were loving, caring, and accepting, and the leaders, Georgia Crosley and Betsy Carpenter, were lifesavers, or at least sanity-savers. Their newsletter was my sounding board for my initial expressions of grief. The Compassionate Friends, Inc. is "a self-help organization offering friendship, understanding, and grief support for bereaved parents, grandparents, siblings, who have experienced the death of a child."

Their Web site is: www.compassionatefriends.org. Their addresses and phone numbers are:

Brazosport Chapter:
321 Linden Lane
Lake Jackson, Texas 77566
(979) 297-8133 and (979) 297-9266
National Headquarters:
P. O. Box 3696
Oak Brook, Illinois 60522-3696
(630) 990-0010 or toll-free (877) 969-0010

Another organization that I have found useful on the internet, although I didn't know about it at the time I had Karen, is Support Organization For Trisomy 18, 13, and Related Disorders (S.O.F.T). It is "a nonprofit volunteer organization offering support for parents who have had a child with a chromosome disorder, and education to families and professionals interested in the care of these children." Their statistics and other information will be much more current than the ones I received when Karen was alive.

Their Web site is: www.trisomy.org. Their E-mail address is: barbsoft@aol.com. Their address and phone numbers are:

SOFT USA
Barb Vanherreweghe
2982 South Union Street
Rochester, New York 14624
(716) 594-4621 or toll-free (800) 716-SOFT (7638)

Another resource, The Arc of the Capital Area, "has been providing services to children and adults with mental retardation and other developmental disabilities and their families in Austin, Texas and surrounding communities since 1949." Their vision is "a future in which people with all disabilities and their families have the same opportunities as others to pursue full and productive lives." Although they provide a wide variety of services through several different programs, my personal experience has been volunteering with their Pilot Parent program, under the excellent supervision of Tammy Mann. For further information, their Web site is: www.arcofthecapitalarea.org. Their address and phone number are:

> The Arc of the Capital Area
> 2818 San Gabriel
> Austin, Texas 78705
> (512) 476-7044

Finally, my experiences have led me to an interest in working with Early Childhood Intervention (ECI), which helps children during the first three years of life. "The Texas Interagency Council on Early Childhood Intervention (ECI) is the state agency that serves Texas families who have babies and toddlers with disabilities or developmental delays.... ECI supports families to help their children reach their potential."

I received a Bachelor of Arts in December 2001 from the University of Texas, with a major in Psychology and a minor in ECI. For information on ECI in Texas, their Web site is: www.eci.state.tx.us. Their address and phone number are:

> ECI
> 4900 North Lamar
> Austin, Texas 78751-2399
> (800) 250-2246

Bibliography

Aspin, Sean. *Rudy*. Directed by David Anspaugh. Columbia/Tristar Studios, 1993.

Bosworth, F.F. *Christ the Healer*. Old Tappan, New Jersey: Fleming H. Revell Company, 1983.

Carroll, Bruce. "Sometimes Miracles Hide." *Sometimes Miracles Hide*. Produced by Brown Bannister and Tom Hemby for RBI Productions. Irving, Texas: Word, Inc., 1991.

Clayman, Charles B., MD, Medical Editor. *The American Medical Association Home Medical Encyclopedia*. New York: Random House, 1989.

Cowan, Mrs. Charles E. *Streams in the Desert*. Grand Rapids, Michigan: Daybreak Books by Zondervan Publishing House, 1965.

Dobson, James Dr. *Dr. Dobson Answers Your Questions*. Wheaton, Illinois: Living Books Edition, Tyndale House Publishers, Inc., 1988.

Francisco, Don. "Love Is Not a Feeling." *Early Works*. 1991.

Hagin, Kenneth. *The Word of Faith*. Tulsa, Oklahoma: RHEMA Bible Church AKA Kenneth Hagin Ministries.

Hagin, Kenneth. *Don't Blame God*. Tulsa, Oklahoma: Kenneth Hagin Ministries.

Hagin, Kenneth. *Love Never Fails*. Tulsa, Oklahoma: Kenneth Hagin Ministries.

Michelmore, Peter. "The Boy Who Surprised Everyone." *Reader's Digest*, July 1991, pp. 63-68.

Rogers, Dale Evans. *Angel Unaware*. Old Tappan, New Jersey: Fleming H. Revell Company, 1984

Taber, Clarence Wilbur. *Taber's Cyclopedic Medical Dictionary*, 11th Edition. Philadelphia: F. A. Davis Company, 1971.

"Voice of the People." *The Brazosport Facts*, March 12, 1989.

Endnotes

[1] Most of the medical terms I attempted to describe are actually a combination of definitions from several sources, which I have generally labeled *Combination*. Because many of the terms in the medical books were lengthy and complicated, often I got a layman's definition, or approval of the one I had devised, from my friend, Linda Hoskins, R.N. Otherwise, the books included:

Clarence Wilbur Taber, *Taber's Cyclopedic Medical Dictionary*, 11th Edition (Philadelphia: F. A. Davis Company, 1971).

Charles B. Clayman, MD, Medical Editor, *The American Medical Association Home Medical Encyclopedia* (New York: Random House, 1989).

[2] Combination.

[3] Oral explanations given by Karen's doctors or nurses. (At the hospital and doctors' offices when I had Karen, I usually kept my notebook with me. I wrote down what they said to help me understand what they were talking about.)

[4] Oral explanations by the doctors or nurses.

[5] Combination.

[6] Oral explanations by the doctors or nurses.

[7] Oral explanations by the doctors or nurses.

[8] Taber, p. F-15.

[9] Combination and oral explanation of the doctors or nurses.

[10] Clayman, p.388.

[11] Oral explanations by the doctors or nurses.

[12] Oral explanations by the doctors or nurses.

[13] Clayman, p.519.

[14] Mrs. Charles E. Cowman, *Streams in the Desert* (Grand Rapids, Michigan: Daybreak Books by Zondervan Publishing House, 1965) pp. 17-19.